FROM DARKNESS TO LIGHT

J. KRISHNAMURTI

FROM DARKNESS TO LIGHT

Poems and Parables

THE COLLECTED WORKS OF KRISHNAMURTI

Volume One

HARPER & ROW, PUBLISHERS

SAN FRANCISCO

Cambridge
Hagerstown
Philadelphia
New York

1817

London
Mexico City
São Paulo
Sydney

The Path, privately published in 1923, published by the Star Publishing Trust, 1928; *The Search,* published by the Star Publishing Trust and George Allen & Unwin, 1927; *The Immortal Friend,* published by the Star Publishing Trust and Boni & Liveright, 1928; *The Song of Life,* published by the Star Publishing Trust and Horace Liveright, 1928; *Parables and Prose Poems,* published in the *Star Review* and/or the *International Star Bulletins* between 1927 and 1931.

FIRST EDITION

Designed by Jim Mennick

Library of Congress Cataloging in Publication Data
Krishnamurti, Jiddu, 1895-
  FROM DARKNESS TO LIGHT.
  (His *The collected works of Krishnamurti*; v. 1)
  I. Title.
B5134.K75A1 1980, vol. 1 [PR9499.3.K714] 181'.4s
ISBN 0-06-064832-5   [821]   79-2985

80 81 82 83 84 10 9 8 7 6 5 4 3 2 1

CONTENTS

PREFACE

The Collected Works of J. Krishnamurti, of which this volume is the first, is a true record for posterity of the works of this unique human being whose message represents no known organized religion, philosophy or ideology.

History has often revealed that the life and experiences of a single human being can be of an unusual character from beginning to end and can have a significant influence on the lives of many others all over the earth. This is especially so if that person is unique as a thinker and teacher endeavoring to communicate the truth and meaning of human experiences that reach to the deepest level in all of us, as he has discovered them on his journey in search of the truth about life and living.

In the life of such a being, as in the lives of many artists, there can be different creative periods, arising out of the experiences of a particular time. These may seem to differ widely in expression but are actually rooted in the same inward creative source, reflecting different insights at different periods of life. Some readers will find this to be true of these teachings and writings of J. Krishnamurti that have been published before over a period of sixty years in various parts of the world.

During the more than half a century that Krishnamurti has been a public figure, traveling continually about the world, his message has been heard and read assiduously by thousands of people of all ages who have come to realize that the *traditional* religious, moral and ethical values have failed to bring about a peaceful and happy social order.

Krishnamurti has provided us with a living restatement of truth, love and beauty—the fundamental essence of the truly religious life, a life free of superstition, greed and fear—which is the only source and foundation of lasting happiness for the individual and for peace and order in our world.

K. & R. FOUNDATION

viii   ∞   FROM DARKNESS TO LIGHT

PUBLISHER'S NOTE

J. Krishnamurti is well known throughout the world as a unique thinker and teacher. Many of his public talks and discussions as well as his personal writings have been published from time to time during the past sixty years; but a great number of these earlier publications have been out of print for years.

The K. & R. Foundation, a California corporation, has as one of its purposes the republication, as originally published, of certain of the works of J. Krishnamurti. These will be contained in *The Collected Works of Krishnamurti,* of which this is the first volume.

In all his writings, Krishnamurti touches on the fundamental truth at the core of all religions, but he gives it a new expression understandable in our time. His expression of this unique realization has naturally varied in the course of the years.

There was a time in the very beginning when Krishnamurti expressed himself through poetry and in parables. These poetic writings represent a facet of Krishnamurti that is characterized by the intensity of his feelings and by his passionate appeal to the individual for self-realization of truth, each in his own unique, inimitable way.

In this first volume of his poetry Krishnamurti uses a multitude of similes in describing his feelings that reflect everywhere the beauty and the wonder of nature. The effect of these descriptions is one of immense tenderness and great strength, of love of God and mankind, of acceptance and surrender at the same time. The language of Krishnamurti is that of a seer and a poet—inevitably it touches profoundly the human heart.

NEITHER TIME . . .

Neither time nor space exists for the man who knows the eternal.

Space and time are real for the man who is yet imperfect and space is divided for him into dimensions, time into past, present and future. He looks behind him and sees his birth, his acquisitions, all that he has rejected. That past is being continually modified by the future which is ever being added to it. From the past man turns his eyes to the future where death, the unknown, the darkness, the mystery, await him.

Fascinated by these he can no longer detach himself from them. The mystery of the future holds for him the fulfillment of all his desires, which the past has denied to him, and in his dreams he flies to that brilliant horizon where happiness must exist, where he must seek it.

Fatal error!

No one will ever pierce the infinite mystery of the future—impenetrable in its evanescent illusion—neither magician, prophet nor God! But on the contrary it will be the mystery which will engulf man, which will not let him escape, which will break the mainspring of his life.

Life is not to be approached through the past, nor through the mirage of the future. Life cannot be approached through intermediaries, nor conquered for another.

That discovery can only be made in the immediate present—by the individual for himself and not for others—by the individual who has become the eternal "I." That eternal "I" is created by the perfection of the self—perfection in which all things are contained, even human imperfections. Man, not yet having achieved that condition of life in the present, lives in the past which he regrets, lives in the future where he hopes, but never in the present which he ignores. This is the case with all men.

Balanced between the past and the future, the "I" is poised as a tiger ready to spring, as an eagle ready to fly, as the bow at the moment of releasing the arrow.

This moment of equilibrium, of high tension, is "creation." It is the fullness of all life, it is immortality.

The wind of the desert sweeps away all trace of the traveler.

The sole imprint is the footstep of the present. The past, the future . . . sands blown by the wind.

J. KRISHNAMURTI
1929

THE PATH

PART I

There is not a cloud in the sky; there is not a breath of wind; the sun is pouring down cruelly and relentlessly its hot rays; there is a mist caused by the heat, and I am alone on the road. On both sides of me there are fields melting into the far distant horizon; there is not a blade of grass that is green; there is not a flower breathing in this heartbroken country; everything is withered and parched; all crying with anguish of the untold and unutterable pain of ages. There is not a tree in the vast fields under whose shade a tender thing might grow up smiling, careless of the cruel sun. The very earth is cracked and gaping hopelessly with bared eyes at the pitiless sun.

The sky has lost its delicate blue and it is gray with the heat of many centuries. Those skies must have shed gentle rain, this very earth must have received it, those dead plants, those huddled up bushes, those withered blades of grass must once have quenched their thirst. They are all dead, dead beyond all thought of life. How many centuries ago the soothing drops of rain fell I cannot tell, nor can those hot stones remember when they were happy in the rain, nor those dead blades of grass when they were wet. Everything is dead, dead beyond hope. There is not a sound; awful and fearsome silence reigns. Now and then, there is a groan of immense pain as the earth cracks, and the dust goes up and comes down, lifeless.

Not a living thing breathes this stifling air; all things, once living, are now dead. The wide stream beside the road, which in former ages bubbled with mirth and laughter, satisfying many living things with its delicious cool waters, is now dead; the bed of the stream has forgotten when the waters used to flow over it, nor can those dead fish, whose bleached and delicate skeletons lie open to the blinding light, remember when they swam in couples exposing their exquisite, brilliant colours to the warm and life-giving sun. The fields are covered with the dead of many bygone ages, never can the dead vibrate again with the happy pulse of life. All is gone, all is spent, death has trapped in its cruel embrace all living things, all except me.

I am alone on the road, not a soul in front of me; there may be many behind me, but I do not desire to look back upon the horror of sufferings of the past. On either side of this long and what seems to be an interminable highway of my life, there is desolate waste ever beckoning me to join its miserable quietude—death. In front of me the Path stretches mile after mile, year after year, century after century, white in the blazing, pitiless sun; the road ever mounts, in an imperceptible inclination. The whiteness of this weary Path, with the glittering sun, makes me almost blind; look where I may to rest my tired eyes, there is everywhere that immense ocean of blinding light, blatant in its intensity.

The sun never goes to sleep but ruthlessly sheds his unwelcome and awful heat. The road is not all even, but, here and there, there are parts as smooth as a lake on a calm, peaceful day. This dreary Path is even to the tread, but unexpectedly, like some unsatisfied storm, which suddenly bursts forth to triumph in its joy of destruction, the road is broken up and becomes merciless to the already bleeding feet. I cannot tell when it will again become smooth and encouraging; it may be at the next footstep, or after many years of toil and suffering. This bitter road cares not if it causes pain or pleasure; it is there for me to tread willingly or unwillingly. Who built this road of misfortune I cannot tell, nor can the road mention his name. It has existed for many centuries, nay for many millennia.

Nobody but me has trodden it; it has been cut out for me to walk alone. Companions, friends, brothers, sisters, fathers and mothers have I had, but on this dreadful road they cannot exist. This Path is like the jealous and exacting lover, hating his love to have other friends and other lovers. The road is my inexorable love, and it guards my love jealously, destroying all those who would accompany me or help me. Exacting in all things both small or great, it never releases me from its cruel, kind gaze. It embraces me with a strength that almost chokes me, and laughs with a knowing kindness as my feet bleed; I cannot go away from it, it is my constant and lonely love. I cannot look elsewhere but only at the long interminable Path.

At times it is neither kind nor unkind—indifferent as to whether I am happy or unhappy, whether I am in pain or in ecstasy, whether I am in profound sorrow or in deep adoration, indifferent to all things. It well knows that I cannot leave that enthralling Path, nor can it depart from my sorrow-laden self. We are inseparable; it cannot exist without me nor I without it. We are one, yet I am different.

Like the smile of a sweet spring morn the Path beckons me to walk on it, and like the angry and treacherous ocean it cheats me of my momentary happiness. It holds me as I fall, in blissful embrace, making me forget the sorrow and the suffering of the past, kissing me with the kiss of a tender and loving mother whose only thought is to protect, and when I am in complete oblivion and ecstasy as that of a man who has drunk deep at the fountain of supreme happiness, it wakes me with a rude shock from my happy and ephemeral dream and pushes me roughly to my aching feet.

Cruel and kind is my lonesome friend and lover, unexpected in her hard tyranny and in her delicious love. Does she like me, I do not care; does she dislike me, I do not care, but she is my only companion, nor do I desire any other.

The sun is scorching me and the Path makes me bleed. I leave no footprints on that hard road nor do I see the traces of any human being. So I am the only lover my Path has had and I glory in my exclusiveness and separateness. I suffer unlike others, am happy unlike others, and my obstinacy in loving her is unlike any other lover the world has ever seen. I am breathless in my adoration of her, and no other worshipper can ever lay his sacrifice at her feet with greater willingness and with greater enthusiasm than I can.

There is no follower with greater fanaticism; nor can there exist a greater devotee. Her cruelty only makes me love her more, and her kindness binds me closer and everlastingly to her. We live for each other and I alone can see her dear face, I alone can kiss her hand. No other lover has she besides me, no other friend. As the young bird that bursts forth from its restraining nest with its untried wings to enjoy the freedom and the beauty of the great world, so have I rushed forward on this Path to enjoy the exhilaration of loving her in solitude away from others who might dare to look on her beauteous face.

Many winds of many seasons have battered me, like a dead leaf blown hither and thither by autumnal winds, but I always have wandered back to this enticing Path. Like a wave glittering in the hot ceaseless sunshine have I been dancing to the fierce winds; like a desert which is bound by no mountain, have I lain open to the sun; like the sands of the ocean, have my lives been. Never a peaceful rest, never has contentment filled my soul, never has joy penetrated my very being and never have I been comforted. No smile has ever compensated my longing; no face, sweet and gentle, has brought balm to my aching heart; no kind words have allayed my infinite suffering.

Neither the love of the mother nor the wife nor the child has ever quenched my burning love; but all have deserted me and I have abandoned them all. Like some leprous thing have I wandered, alone and unwept for. Pain and sorrow have been my eternal and inseparable companions. Like a shadow has my grief clung to me; like one in everlasting pain have I wept bitter tears.

Many a time have I longed for death and complete oblivion and neither has been granted to me; many a time have I looked death in its horrible face, tearing my heart and welcoming joyously the terror of so many, but it smiled and gave me a blessing; many a time, tired of wooing death, have I turned my face and footsteps to the altar of love and worship, but little comfort have I found; many a sacrifice, both of myself and of others, have I made in the hope of reaching the altar of contentment, but in vain; many a time have I dwelt in breathless adoration, but, like the scent of a delicately perfumed flower, has my adoration been wafted through centuries and left me listless, and still on my aching knees; many a time have I laid fragrant flowers at sacred feet, and no blessing have I received.

Many a time have I offered to the numerous Gods of many lands and races, but the Gods have always been silent and Their look always averted; many a time have I been Their priest in Their sacred temples but the white robes have fallen off me and left me naked to the sun; many a holy lotus of the temple have I kissed in adoration of the Gods, but the lotus has withered in my hand. Many a time have I worshipped at the altars that the world has ever created, but with bowed head and silent have I returned.

Many ceremonies have I performed, but my longing has never been satisfied; many rites have I delighted in, but there has been no joy, no hope. In many a temple have I been consecrated, but have received no comfort. Many a sacred book have I read, but knowledge was denied to me. Many a life have I spent in holiness, but my life has been dark. Many a window have I opened to gaze at the stars, but they parted not with their profound wisdom. Often have I lain awake looking into nothingness, looking for light, but darkness, intense darkness has ever reigned.

Often, in many lives, have I deliberately followed, sometimes blindly, sometimes with open eyes, the humble teachers of the secluded village, but their teachings have left me at the foot of the lonesome hill. I have lived nobly and toiled laboriously; I have restrained myself and I have been without restraint. Often have I cried, with aching heart and with bitter tears for the Divine Hand to lead me, but no hand has aided me. I have struggled fiercely with humanity to gain the light, but the light and the humanity have I lost. I have meditated profoundly with eyes fixed on the goal, controlling all my emotions, searching for truth; but nothing was revealed to me.

Many a time have I sought seclusion from my noisy brethren and tried to escape from their petty and ignoble thoughts and worries, from their false and uncouth emotions, from their little miseries and sorrows which they have created for themselves, from their cruel hate and their infantile pity, from their puerile affection and their fleeting compassion, from their unfair gossip and from their warm and selfish friendship, from their bitter quarrels and their loud rejoicings, from their vindictive anger and their soft love, from their talk of great things which they know not of, and their knowledge of the little things which they know so well, from their showering honors and their withering scorn, from their gross flattery and their obvious contumely, from their love desires and their petty aversions, from all that was human, and longing for all that was divine, noble and great; but wheresoever I have been, and wheresoever I go, humanity with its terrible agonies and crying pain has pursued me.

Many a time I sought seclusion and solitude in the forest glade dim and peaceful, but I found it peopled with my thoughts and haunted with misery. Many a time have I thrilled at the beauty of the world, the soft spring and the harsh winter, the calm and glorious sunset and the heavenly and luminous stars, the waking morn and the dying evening, the tender moon and the soft light, the pitiless sun and the shadows numberless, the green grass, the velvety leaf, the fierce tiger, the gentle deer, the loathsome reptile, the dignified elephant, the magnificent mountains, the boisterous seas. I have enjoyed to the full the beauties that the world can give, but no joy have I found in them. I have wandered in the shady valleys and climbed the precipitous mountains. I have searched everywhere in vain and in pain.

Many a time, in many a life, have I practiced Yoga through starvation, through physical torture, through self-denial, but I have not seen the seated God. Desires and false emotions have I annihilated; I have lived purely according to the sacred laws of many nations, I have done noble deeds which the world has praised and honoured, and it has showered me with earthly glories. I have never bowed my bleeding head to sorrow nor to temptation, and I have made pilgrimages to the earth's heavenly abodes; but always and everywhere have I found no true and lasting comfort.

Visions have I had in the temples of Nineveh, Babylon, Egypt, and in the sacred temples of holy India; their Gods have I worshipped, denying earthly happiness, renouncing father, mother, wife and child, offering sacrifices great and small, noble and petty, sacrificing my body and my very soul for the light to guide me; contentment has been denied me in all things I have done.

I have loved divinely, I have suffered nobly, I have smiled joyously, I have danced rapturously in front of many Gods, I have been intoxicated with divinity, I have longed to be freed from this aching world. I have helped many though helping I needed most; I have healed many though healing I needed most; I have guided many though guidance I needed most; I have comforted when comfort I needed most. When in deep sorrow I have smiled, when joyous, I have grieved; losing, I was happy; gaining, I was miserable; and ever have I loved my God.

Yet my soul is in utter chaos, yet I am pitiably blind, surrounded by darkness and unrealities, yet the pure light is denied me, yet healing comfort have I none, yet soothing contentment is withheld, yet blissful happiness is nowhere to be found, and I am alone, lonely as a fair wanderer in the sky. I am alone with myself.

Tired of worship and adoration, tired of solitude and loneliness, tired of seeking and longing for divine happiness, tired of sacrifice and self-mortification, tired of searching for the light and the truth, tired of being noble and unselfish, tired of the struggle and the steep climb, tired of body and soul, I threw myself with a vigour and an uproar on to the material world, hoping thus to gain the ungainable and unfathomable.

I became young and healthy, beautiful and passionate, free and joyous, gay with not a thought for the morrow, carefree and careless. I set about diligently and systematically to enjoy myself supremely and selfishly, heeding nothing but bodily pleasure and flashes of mental enjoyment. I set about to gain and to taste every experience both low and high that the mortal world could give me; nothing could be withheld from me, supreme pleasure was my sole aim.

Often I was born rich to sleep in the lap of luxury and to enjoy the lull of flattery. Youth was on my side and beauty was not denied to me; with these two the world and its gross and unappetising pleasures were ever open to me. Foremost in all that was boisterous and lively was I; the untold pleasures of youth had I from morning till night, nay till gentle dawn appeared in the dim east, surrounded by licentious youth. I was foremost in gaiety, no rival could I find in my extremes. The pleasures of bright Nineveh, of gay Babylon, of wondrous Egypt and sun-burnt India, were ever at my call. I was showered with their honours, with their praise and their flattery. I drank deep the wine of merriment at the fountain of gaiety and satisfaction.

Slaves and servants had I many, but never a master, not one. Desires, springing up like the glorious flowers of the tender spring, were immediately satisfied, never was there a curb to my whims and caprices. No sooner was there a thought of enjoyment, it was fulfilled at the next pleasurable moment. Love, of all kinds, was ever at my elbow; no pure thing was safe from me. I desecrated all chastity, scoffing at the high gods, spurning the humbly faithful of the human race. Rich and fragrant wine was always beside me with a slave to hand it to me.

Surfeited with the throbs of gratification of man, in all the civilized countries, among all refined nations and races, I incarnated as a woman to relish the delicate raptures of being loved by passionate men. Never was I satisfied with the monotony of one lover and the love of one wooer, but many and innumerable adorers had I at my window. Languishing in my love, clamoring for more, I passed my life. All the sufferings of child-bearing, the joys of having a child, the grief of losing one, the pains and sorrows of old age and the neglect and indifference of former lovers, have I experienced, and have gloated over past memories, and cried over long lost admirers.

Many a life, tired of licentious and free-loving woman, I became a sacred wife and gained the happiness of pure love. Children have I borne with pleasure and there never stirred in my heart, as of yore, the hate of suffering when I brought forth to the world an innocent being. The tender love of clinging children, their innocent smiles, their little sorrows and pains, their pure hearts, their dear and holy kisses, their delicate embraces, have I enjoyed, and have been thrilled at their welcome.

A loving wife, a tender mother I became, and gloried in the feelings of love. Having gained that experience of womanhood, I turned once more to the free man with strong and brutal emotions. Passion rent my heart and I lay in the lap of luxury forgetful of sorrow and pain, oblivious to the suffering of any creature. I lived a life of selfish enjoyment, rich in gross experiences, wealthy in mortal pleasures, and the material world withheld nothing from me.

But there was no satisfaction, no contentment, no blissful happiness, and my heart was as bare and desolate as the waste desert with no living thing to give beauty and rapture to it.

I had tasted the wealth of the worlds, and I became a poor man, a beggar, wandering from house to house, denied and cursed at, dirty, tired, ugly, hideous in my own eyes, laughed and pointed at, hungry, fatherless, motherless, with no woman who dared to touch me, pitiable, riddled with known and unknown diseases, with bleeding feet; with a dirty sackcloth on my shoulders which served me as a robe on festal days, as a blanket when the cool night breezes blew, as a headgear when the blazing sun shone pitiless on my dirty head; and with a worn staff in my hand have I wandered through the rich and inhospitable streets of many nations. The wealthy shopkeepers welcomed me, each and all, when I was born in their gorgeous cities, with a curse and a howl, with a hit and a kick; I was chased by men and savage dogs.

With faces averted the people passed, and their hands withheld the comfort which lay in their power to give. The villages and towns were alike; pitiless and with a hard heart the peoples of all nations passed me by. My bedchamber was some desolate and lonesome spot where no man or animal dared to come, loathing to breathe such foul air. Hunger always gnawing at my stomach, heat of the sun always burning me, cold winds of the north always biting me, frosts withering me, shivering with ague and pain, tottering with weariness, eaten by disease, have I wandered all over the earth, never meeting a smile, never a kind word, never a loving look.

The dogs were happy; they were fed, they had someone to pet them, to comfort and care for them; but even the dogs howled at me. No house ever opened its door to my occasional knock; the holy priests chased me from their sacred temples. Children, stricken with horror, stopped crying when they beheld me. Mothers have held their infants closer at the distant sight of me, rushing with a shriek into their protecting homes.

I seemed to spread pestilence and unhappiness; the very heavens clouded. The rivers dried up at my approach, as I went to quench my thirst; the trees gave me no fruit; the earth quaked at my advance and the stars disappeared at the sight of my unfortunate being. No gentle rain fell on my head, cleansing my impurities.

Thus for many generations, among various nations, among strange people, alone and unhappy, like a lone cloud that hangs over the vale and the hill, that is chased and harried by wanton winds, have I wandered, miserable and loathed.

Shelter and physical comfort have I not found for many ages; weary of body and desolate of soul, hunted like some vicious animal, have I sought seclusion, and in solitude, alas! misery ever dwelt with me. Like a dead leaf that is crushed by many a foot, have I suffered within this cruel and gruesome abode of the flesh, poor and dirty, without love and without hate, with complete indifference as to sorrow or pain, void of intelligence, famished and thirsty, all the glorious emotions that once kindled my heart dead for many an age. Blind of hope, despairing of my existence, crawling from human sight, detested and loathed by the youngest of humanity, have I sought, through this agony and through this interminable sorrow, through this torture of the physical body and through the privation of the soul, through this degradation and horror —crying and in eternal pain, for that light, for that comfort and for that happiness which was denied to me when sunk in gross riches, when wallowing in selfish contentment and caring for nothing except for my crude pleasures, which was withheld from me also when I attempted to lead the pure and noble life.

For when I worshipped and dwelt in pure adoration, when life was a continual self-denial and self-mortification, when sin was abhorred by me, when, with head erect, I gazed always into the dim future for truth, when there was so much light around me, and yet profound and dismal darkness within me, when I loved purely and longed nobly, when I was thrilled at the simple name of God; in those lives of temple piety and harmlessness, no blissful contentment could I find.

PART II

Many and varied were my experiences, thoughts and emotions; innumerable passions, bestial and noble, fine sympathies and great loves; many a love, pure and selfish, many shades of gratification and fine and glorious feelings, much high intelligence and low cunning have I known; through many ages and through many centuries, through different nations and races, through every capacity, have I passed and gained the knowledge that the world can give to one who seeks and suffers.

Yet where is that light which sages have seen, that truth which conquers all unrealities, that compassion which heals all suffering, that blissful contentment which brings eternal happiness to the sorrow-stricken soul and that wisdom which guides the aching humanity? Wheresoever I have been, wheresoever I have groped, I have returned with an empty hand and grieving heart. Like an erring child that strays from its beloved mother, have I wandered far into the realms of despair and unrealities seeking the great reality, far from the lonely road have I departed in quest of that unconquerable longing and that unquenchable thirst; but I have been burnt with anguish, and with drooping head have I returned.

No satisfaction or gratification have I found either amidst warring humanity or away from the madding crowd; happy or unhappy, elevated or degraded, in pain or in pleasure, there has always dwelt with me, like the dark shadow, a deep void which nothing could fill, an infinite longing which could not be satisfied; I have wandered blindly and wearily, asking every passer-by for that balm which would cure my aching heart; they gave of their best with a gentle smile and a blessing, but did not further my long quest. Where is that light and where is that infinite happiness?

I am tired, tired with the wanderings of innumerable ages; I am weary, weary with the fatigue of many centuries; I am exhausted from lack of strength to struggle and to fight. My feet falter at each footstep; I can scarce drag myself along; I am almost blind with long and continuous use of my eyes through interminable eras; I am hairless, haggard and old. Pride and youth have gone from me; I am bent double with the weight and sorrow of my infinite pain; beauty, of which I once clamorously boasted, has deserted me and left me a monstrous horror. What has passed and what has been wrought through those long and insufferable years is beyond my memory, and my indifference is complete.

I am desireless; no passion sways me; no affections tear me; emotions have lost their ancient and all-powerful influence over me; tender love is behind me far back in the distance; the exhilaration of action has been killed out of me; ambition, that spurs so many, either bringing laurels or dishonor, glory or shame, is buried in the distant past; pride that holds its head high amidst turmoil of noble and ignoble deeds, is vanished, never to reappear; fear, that overwhelms and holds men in thrall, is crushed; gruesome death, the awful and impartial companion of all, can no longer dismay me with its threatening stare. Yet there is a deep void of discontent and an everlasting longing for the almost unattainable.

Can I ever reach the mountain top of blissful contentment and grasp the supreme happiness? Oh! Mighty Beings, have compassion on the lonely traveler who has voyaged through many stormy seas, traveled through many lands and passed through many sorrows! I am alone—come to my help ye pitying and happy Beings! I have worshipped You, I have adored You, I have offered many a sacrifice at Your altars, and much have I endured to kiss Your sacred feet. Comfort me, Ye Masters of Wisdom, with those eyes of love and understanding. What have I done, and what must I do to reach the glory and the greatness? How long must this pitiable condition last? How long, oh Master, ere I behold Thy sacred beauty? How long must I walk on this long and lonely Path? Is there an end to this interminable agony which burneth the very love for Thee? Why hast Thou turned away Thy rapturous face, and whither has gone that beatific smile that allays all suffering in all things?

I have served the Great Ones and the needy world in a humble and despairing way; I have loved in a blind fashion all things, both small and great, and I have drunk at all the fountains of earthly wisdom. Never have I reached Thy feet. Like a glorious flower that has withered, that has lost its fragrance, its beauty and its tenderness, is the existence of my life; cheerless and desolate, like a dead tree that gives no cool shade to the weary traveler, I have given all, withholding nothing, and empty and hopeless have I remained. I have led the blind and the sorrow-stricken, myself being blind and sorrow-stricken. Why hast Thou not stretched Thy helping hand when I have stumbled? I am weary with asking; I have no hope; all seems to be dead, and utter darkness prevails. No tears fall, but yet I am crying, crying in infinite pain. No passer-by can help me in my pitiable plight, for there is no one but me on this long, long Path that winds about like a mighty stream without a beginning and without an end. Desperate, like a madman, I wander on, knowing not whither to go, nor caring what becomes of me. The sun can no longer burn me. I am burnt to the very bone. Like a vast ocean which is boundless, is the glaring whiteness that surrounds me on all sides, and I can scarce distinguish the Path which leads me to my ultimate happiness. Everything is left behind me: my companions, my friends and my love—I am desperately lonely.

Oh! Master of Compassion, come to my rescue and lead me out of this profound darkness to pure light, and to the haven of immortality, and to the peaceful enlightenment. I seek the pure enlightenment that few Great Beings have attained. I seek the high Deliverer who will free me from this wheel of birth and death. I seek the Brother that will share with me His divine wisdom; I seek the Lover that will comfort me; I seek to lay my weary head in the lap of Compassion; I seek the Friend that will guide me; I seek to take refuge in the Light.

The Path gives no answer to my desperate calling; the cruel skies look down on me with complete indifference; the comforting echo does not exist, nor is there the dismal moan of many winds. Profound silence reigns, save for the monotonous sound of slow breathing and the dragging of weary footsteps. There is no peace; there is a movement of thousands of invisible beings around me, as though they were mocking at my solitary suffering. The expectant hush that comes before a storm is my sole companion; only the annihilation of centuries replies to my continuous entreaties; isolation is complete and cruel.

The Path no longer speaks to me as of ancient days when she used to point out the right and the wrong, the true from the false, the essential from the unessential, the great from the petty. Now she is as silent as the grave. She has shown me a part of the way; but the rest I must tread by myself, before this beloved Path must be left behind when I reach the mightier and more glorious Path. She cannot enter there, she cannot be the signpost as of yore, but let me be satisfied with the thought of her guidance through many epochs and storms to that everlasting resting-place.

The Path lies in front of me, gently and imperceptibly climbing, with never a curve and not a thing to obstruct its gentle slope. Like some gigantic snake, whose head and tail are unapproachable, whose eyes cannot perceive the end of its being, that lays itself in warm sand, heavy with killing, sleepy and contented, is the silent Path.

It appears to be breathing and sighing with some quiet and happy satisfaction, but now the sun steadily pours down his burning rays and drives away all thought from my mind. My only longing is to find some delightful cool shade where I could rest my weary body for a while; but an irresistible force pushes me and urges me on, never allowing me any respite. That power impels me to go forward with faltering footsteps. I cannot resist it. I am weak and exhausted, but I obey that eternal and powerful compelling. I take a step, totter and fall, like a swift bird that is wounded by the cruel arrow; I struggle and become unconscious. Slowly and wearily I wake up and gaze at the naked and bright heavens, and I desire to lie and rest where I am; but that mighty force pushes me onto my feet, as of yore, to walk on the never-ending Path.

Lo, there is a solitary tree, many feet away, whose delicious shadow welcomes me. The leaves are tender, velvety, and fresh, as though the sudden healing breath of spring had but lately awakened the dead branches to joyous life and to delicate green foliage. Its shadow is thick, shutting out the searching sun. The fresh fragrant grass and the protecting tree smile with contentment on me, inviting me to share their happy abode. It is full of birds, joyous in their continuous chatter, calling to each other in playful tones. With failing strength I drag myself to enjoy the rare gift which the kind gods have granted to me.

As I with pain approach, the whole tree bends down welcoming me, giving some of its vital strength; I crawl under its fragrant and whispering shadow and gaze wearily into its cool depths. Sleep and exhaustion overcome me; I am asleep, lulled by the welcome twitterings of many birds and the gentle rustle of many leaves. I rest through happy moments of complete oblivion of all suffering and pain, and the ache of many ages. Might I lie here, always, in this soft light, soothed by the murmurings of living things, unruffled by inner and outer storms! Glorious would it be to lie everlastingly here and sleep, sleep, sleep. . . . .

I am burning, the sun is viciously glaring on me, revengeful of my momentary happiness. Where is my beloved tree and where are those happy birds with their happy song? Gaze as I may, nowhere can I find the tree of happiness. Gone, gone, and I am alone once again. Was it a dream? Was it the ancient unreality, taking a form that would give sure delight? Was it the pity of some kind God, or the cruel sport of a God unkind? Was it the great promise of the future? Or was it that some mighty Being desired to test the strength of my forbearance? Many vanishing realities have I followed only to hear their merciless laughter when I have grasped them; but here I thought that I was safe from their old and bitter sway, their barbarous persecution when I sought the lasting—the real. They have, then, pursued me even into this far and lonely place? With infinite caution have I learned to disentangle the real from the false, and when I thought I had mastered the supreme art, must I begin again at the bottom of the difficult ladder?

When I commenced this Path in the bygone ages, there was a firmness in my tread; now again decision rules my steps, a new enthusiasm is born in me, as of yore, when before the many sufferings and many sorrows I was eager to face the unknown, and anxious to test my strength against the unweary Path. The joy of struggle is surging up in me to conquer the mighty and immortal happiness. The Path with its great force need no longer impel me forward; I run faster, nor do my feet falter. I no longer lag behind. I am the Master of the Path. No longer need it spur me to act, for I am action; I am willing and I walk in freedom.

The Path stretches mile upon mile, age upon age; steeper than of yore, narrower, more strenuous, the way winds precipitously, leaving behind the country of the past. Far below me lies the land of desolation and of immense sorrow, where Unreality, in many shapes and in many a guise, rules the great stricken dominions. Here, at this altitude, there reigns complete silence; the silence smiles on me; but as I walk unceasingly on this mountainous way, the recent joy is dead again, my weary feet falter as of old, and I long for that beloved tree which shared with me its happy shade and the soft wooing songs of the innumerable birds.

That phantom tree gave me but the happiness of a fleeting moment, and yet I was gratified with that temporary joy. I beseech the same God who extended his fitful compassion over me, to grant me but a moment of shade, the happy song to lull the aching heart, and the companionship. If it was a dream of fantasy, let me once more embrace it and cling to it even though it be for a brief space! Though ephemeral was the taste of that momentary pleasure, grateful was the rest in the deep, cool shadows.

Where art thou, my beloved, glorious unreality though thou be? Hast thou forgotten the weary traveler who sheltered in thy calm shade? Though thou hast been a false comfort, yet how I crave for thee, to sink once more in thy soft arms, forgetting all but my delicious comfort. Grant me thyself but this once, and I shall be thy love everlasting. I am weary; come to my aid, my beloved, with thy transient beauty. Lull me with thy false murmurings, and encourage me with thy untrue flattery. I am spent with beseeching and exhausted with weariness, and I am in utter despair.

Far in the distance, there is a clump of trees surrounding a gay house, with a sweet and fragrant garden. I am in it enjoying the cool, and the bewitching smiles of many a beauteous maiden. I join in their fresh laughter and in their merry-making. Their pleasure-laden voices soothe me and the soft music lulls me to sleep. Here there is peace and quietness and complete forgetfulness. I am happy and contented, for in this abode of pleasure is the joy for which I have searched through innumerable ages; reality cannot exist but here. Am I not satisfied? Am I not surrounded by all that I desire? Why did I endure, why did I struggle? For here is balm to the aching heart and comfort to the comfortless.

How long, or how many ages, or how many days, I have dwelt in this pleasurable abode, I cannot tell; nor can I count the happy hours that have been spent here. Once again the unquenchable longing is stirring in the depths of my heart; it has awakened anew and tortures me. I cannot rest in this house of gratification; the contentment which it promised has not been given to me; there is no happiness, no comfort within its walls. I have been deceived with unrealities; I have feasted on untruth; I have been guided by the light of false reason, and I have worshipped, as of yore, at the temple of darkness. I have cheated myself with the temporary and the impermanent; after many ages and much pain have I once again fallen a victim to the mocking gods. Again must I wander forth; again must I face the unyielding Path.

Once more I am in the blazing sun, once more do I feel the strength to face the long journey. Fresh enthusiasm and fresh hopes are surging in me; courage is born anew. The Path of many ages smiles on me, promising once more to be the passage of light. Like a mighty tree that has bowed down before the stormy winds, but reasserts itself when they are stilled, and gazes again, with head erect, into the unfathomable skies, defiant and sparkling in the sun, so do I feel. Once more the joy of loneliness is pulsating through all my being, and the solitude, away from vain pleasures and the unmeaning crowd, is like a breath of fresh wind that blows from the mountains. I am alive once more eager to find the end of all sorrow, the glorious liberation. Happy is the man who struggles!

PART III

The long sinuous Path lies in front of me, and all life has ceased to exist except for the one traveler on that lonely road.

I am throbbing with the excitement of a new and strenuous conquest, like a general, proud and haughty, that marches into a vanquished town. I long for greater and more difficult battles to be won, and I cry for the lack of them.

The solemn stillness breaks in upon my joy, and the grave quietness grips me. I am humbled by the vast expanse, and the pitiless skies threaten me; the pride of victory is broken, and its glory has departed; the terrible loneliness is gently and slowly overwhelming me. But the longing to attain the end is unabated; invincible is the strength, and the will to succeed is indomitable.

For how many centuries I have traveled I cannot count for my memory is weary, but I have journeyed through many seasons. The Path is as tired as he who treads it, and both are crying for the end, but both are willing, the one to lead, the other to follow.

On either side of the road there arise in the far distance, at fitful intervals, tall and stately trees, tossing their bright heads in the sun, forgetting that they were like plants once upon a time. Birds of all feathers, of all hue and of all sizes, frequent them; their plaintive but happy cries reach my ears that have not heard a sound for many an age, except the sound of weary footsteps.

As I approach those joyous creatures they are not afraid, but gaze with supreme indifference, continuing their songs. Under the shade, the green grass sways to the soft music of the wind among the leaves. The strong tree, the gay birds, and the humble grass, all welcome me and promise to lull me to sleep. It is so close, so fragrant, so peaceful to the worn eyes—I almost hesitatingly yield—but there arise in me the memories of other trees, other birds and other shades so deliciously welcoming, yet so deceitful. My beloved Path smiles, watching and wondering what my actions will be, whether I shall choose again the shadows.

It is cool under that tree, and blissful with the song of the birds and the soft music of the rustling leaves. Ah! let me stay but a fleeting moment and then let me pass on! The sun is hot and I am weary, and my body aches with the long journey. The refreshing shadows can do me no harm—let me but stay, Oh, thou inexorable Path, for a happy second! Long sleepless nights have I passed with thee for many centuries, and dost thou grudge and deny me the sleep of but a passing moment? Canst thou not grant me this one pitiable desire? Whither hath fled thy love, thy infinite understanding? I implore thee not to turn away from me, but to answer to my call.

A profound silence reigns. The wind has ceased to play with the leaves. The birds are quiet, quiet as death, and the mighty tree broods in deep thought. The shadows have deepened, there prevails a greater calm and greater cool; the green, tender grasses look on me with their small inquisitive eyes, debating in their little minds as to the cause of my unforeseen faltering, whispering to each other in encouragement at my plight. The Path of many experiences and great understanding smiles on my struggling hesitation, with neither encouragement nor pleasure; it is a smile of wisdom and of knowledge, which says: "Thou mayest do what thou desirest, but repentance awaits thee."

My choice is made. Like morning mist that is gently dispelled by the first warm rays of the slow-rising sun, so the magnificent tree of gratification fades gradually before me; the gay birds melt away as before a fast-approaching storm, and the green grass withers in the burning heat of the sun. There remains only a faint vestige of the past. The Path leads on and I humbly follow.

At irregular intervals along the roadside there arise trees, inviting me to taste of their bright-colored and luscious fruit and enjoy its sweetness. It would soothe my parched throat and quench my burning thirst, but my Path is rigorous, and I pass them by. Further on there are magnificent houses, places of pleasure and delight, their welcoming doors always open inviting the travel-worn pilgrim. An age and many lives lie between house and house, and the tired traveler is the too-willing victim of their charm. Craving for their enchanting shelter, many a time have I hesitated at their doorsteps, sometimes straying into them and coming out with shame to walk again with gladness on the clean, sunburnt path.

The house of strong and selfish passions, with its gross gratifications and its impurities, have I entered, and have feasted on all that they could give. Oft have I passed with lingering footsteps the house of many false shadows, the house of satiety with its fleeting contentment, the house of flattery, and the house of learning, where false and fugitive facts lull the ignorant; but only to be enticed into the house of the love that limits, that is selfish, that is unkind, forgetting all except the one; the love that clings, the love that desires; the narrow love of the father, of the mother, the sister, the brother, and the child; the love that slowly and pitilessly destroys the nobler feelings; the love that contents itself with little things.

Many a time have I crossed the threshold of the house of blissful ignorance, of the brilliant house of vain flattery, and of the dismal house of black hate and cunning deceit. Often have I fallen to the temptations of the imperishable house of intolerance, to the boisterous house of patriotism, that breeds venomous and warring hate, and the house of solitary and cold pride, that is unapproachable and untouchable. In the house of friendship that uproots the friendship of others and is consumed with jealousy, and in the house of concealed and talented vice, have I sojourned for many weary seasons. And I have visited the house of small wisdom that excludes all knowledge except of its own petty creation, and the house of little learning that understands little but condemns violently and clamorously all that is beyond its insignificant comprehension.

Many a house of religion have I entered, dwelling within its narrow walls, sleeping in the lap of dark superstition, worshipping false gods, sacrificing innocent things at the temple's altars, and taking part in futile, religious wars and bitter persecution. Wandering into dark houses, have I sought light, and have strayed forth blind and comfortless.

The sympathetic Path ever understood me when I returned to its bare arms, with head bowed down, with shame gnawing at my heart; it ever welcomed me, promising to be my guide and my everlasting friend.

I can see on each side of the long pathway many temptations in delightful shapes and forms, but they are not for me. Let others be enticed, but I will follow my ancient Path. My sore need is to rest and to drink deep at the long-promised source, and no longer do I desire to quench my immemorial thirst at the shadowy fountains. Yet, as far as the eye can see, false things obstruct my view. Once I was able to talk quietly and for many an hour with my lonely companion, the Path, but now it is silent, overwhelmed by sound. Once there was profound peace and tranquillity, but now the holy silence is broken by the barbarous tongues of the multitude. Yet through these clamorous scenes and continuous babble my Path leads, and I follow without hesitation.

How long I have traveled through the land of false fantasies I cannot say, but unerring, with a grave deliberation, have I adhered to my pathway. Always the Path mounts, and with aching limbs have I climbed, clinging desperately; but never have I strayed and gone down into the dark valley. Many centuries have I struggled, resisting fleeting pleasures and inclinations; and yet in front of me there ever springs up temptation in new and varied forms to beguile me.

True it is that I can never again be their victim, and yet. . . . . Ye pitiless gods, is there never an end to this goading misery and to this cruel and false land of passing desires? For how many an age have I trod this Path of righteousness! Yet the end is still not in view. Or is this the goal of all my endurance? Nay, it cannot be, for I have seen, once upon a time, in a far bygone age, the summit of enlightenment. But for how many incarnations must I wander amidst sorrow and tribulation before I knock at the portals of bliss? Without demand, without question, and without lamentation, I must tread this Path for another age.

I am weary and sick at heart; incarnations of great misery and pain have I endured. Vain hopes and promises have made me strong; imperishable has been my desire for the goal; persistent has been my blind groping after truth, and indestructible my ardent enthusiasm. Can all my aching sorrow and my torture be in vain? Cannot my beloved Path lead me to the mountain top, as it has constantly and faithfully promised? Still, after the exquisite pain and indescribable longing, does the pathway lead amidst a vast expanse of shadowy illusions. Why? Ah! what have I done and what have I left undone, what little things of life have I neglected, what sacrifices are there still to be offered, what still greater agonies must I bear? What still greater purifications must I undergo, what still fiercer burning must I sustain, and what still mightier experience of torture awaits me before I reach that abode of pure enlightenment and sacred content?

The mother who bore me knew not what she did, and, had she known, the milk that she nourished me with so tenderly would have turned to poison, and would have spared me these never-ending tortures. Happy would I have been to cease upon the midnight hour, but idle is it to moan and hurl myself against the inevitable. Blameless is my dear mother, and fruitlessly do I clamor against the pain of evolution. And in the end this groping must cease, this fumbling in the dark; for the door of knowledge must be found; there must be the light that guides, the truth that gives contentment, the enlightenment that brings calm happiness.

Oh! I can no longer cry, my body is too feeble to stand, the strength is gradually ebbing out of me—my entire being revolts against the merciless void. Can no god turn his pitiful eyes on the lonesome, spent traveler? Ye Masters of Wisdom, have compassion and shed that infinite mercy that can heal and that can bring light to the wanderer in utter darkness. O, ye cool nights, compel the fiery sun to depart hence and, ye dark clouds, cover up the burning rays! Ah! for the strong hand that could lead and support me, the gentle voice that could comfort and encourage me, the embrace and the kiss that could make me forget! Forlorn am I and with a dying voice, I call . . .

The voice of profound quietness answers me with complete silence, and the void echoes that dreadful stillness. My beloved Path smiles on me, but, pitifully and on all sides, even among the boisterous houses of mirth, deep and awful quiet reigns, as on a night when some murderous deed is being enacted or when the churchyard grave opens its ponderous jaws as in a subdued yawn. I am exhausted, and I totter. The end of my very being draweth nigh. Within the mind's eye I seem to perceive the vision of the haven of perfect peace and the resting-place for the weary and the travel-worn. Yet for how many an age must I still endure this pain of the mind, this surging dissatisfaction, this grief of ages and these woes of bodily suffering, I cannot tell. As far as the eye can scan, I see nothing but shifting and transient things. Yet at each footstep there throbs in me the assurance that the end of the long journey is at hand and approacheth like a ship at sea. May the deities that be above hasten me towards my destination!

Suddenly the air has become still, breathless with some great expectation, and there is a hush like that which comes for a moment after a glorious sunset, when the whole world is in profound adoration. There is a deep silence as on a night when the distant stars waft their kisses to each other, there is an unexpected tranquillity as that of a sudden cessation in a thunderous storm, and there reigns a great peace as in the precincts of a sacred temple. Within me the pain and sorrow of ages is partly stilled; there is a faint and soothing murmuring in the air as my eyes softly close. All things animate and inanimate are resting from their weary toil. The whole world is peacefully asleep and dreaming sweet dreams. The sun, whose fiery rays have for so many ages burnt me ruthlessly, has suddenly become kind, and there is a coolness as that of a deep wooded forest. Divinity is taking shape within me.

The Path has become much steeper and I feebly climb the difficult ascent. As I mount this hill, the abodes of innumerable pleasures of the flesh, the houses of many desires and the green trees grow scarce, and as I reach the summit the enticing fantasies entirely vanish. The Path ever ascends in a long straight line, the air is cooler and the climbing is easier. There is a fresh energy born within me and I surge forward with renewed enthusiasm.

Far in the high distance my Path vanishes into a thick grove of mighty and ancient trees. I dare not look behind or on either side, for the pathway has become precipitous and dangerously narrow. I traverse this perilous passage in a spent and dreamy condition, with my eyes ever fixed on the far-off vision, scarcely looking or caring where I tread. I am in great ecstasy, for the dim sight ahead of me has inspired a deep and lasting hope. With a light footstep I am running forward, fearful lest the happy image should dissolve and elude me, as it has done so often. There is not another traveler in front of me, but the pathway is smooth as though worn by thousands of footsteps through innumerable ages; it shines like a mirror; it is slippery. I tread as though walking in sleep, dreading to wake to false realities and transient things. The vision stands out clear and more distinct as I rapidly approach.

The gracious Gods have at last answered my pitiful calls uttered in the wilderness. My long and sorrowful journey has come to an end and the glorious journey has begun. Far ahead there are other Paths and other gateways, at whose doors I shall knock with greater assurance and with a more joyous and understanding heart. From this height I can behold all the Paths that lie below me. They all converge to this point, though separated by immeasurable distances; many are the travelers on these lonely Paths, but yet each traveler is proud in his blind loneliness and foolish separation. For there are many who follow him and many who precede him. They have been like me, lost in their own narrow path, avoiding and pushing aside the greater road. They struggle blindly in their ignorance, walking in their own shadow and, clinging desperately to their petty truths, they call forth despairingly for the greater truth.

My Path that has guided me through rough and storm-laden countries is beside me. I am gazing with welling tears at those weary and sorrow-eyed travelers. My beloved, my heart is broken at the cruel sight; for I cannot descend and give them divine water to quench their vehement thirst. For they must find the eternal source for themselves.

But, ye merciful Gods, can I at least make their path smoother and alleviate the pain and the sorrow which they have created for themselves through ignorance and pitiful carelessness!

Come all ye that sorrow, and enter with me into the abode of enlightenment and into the shades of immortality. Let us gaze on the everlasting light, the light which gives comfort, the light which purifies. The resplendent truth shines gloriously and we can no longer be blind, nor is there need to grope in the abysmal darkness. We shall quench our thirst, for we shall drink deep at the bubbling fountain of wisdom.

I am strong, I no longer falter; the divine spark is burning in me; I have beheld in a waking dream, the Master of all things and I am radiant with His eternal joy. I have gazed into the deep pool of knowledge and many reflections have I beheld. I am the stone in the sacred temple. I am the humble grass that is mown down and trodden upon. I am the tall and stately tree that courts the very heavens. I am the animal that is hunted. I am the criminal that is hated by all. I am the noble that is honoured by all. I am sorrow, pain and fleeting pleasure; the passions and the gratifications; the bitter wrath and the infinite compassion; the sin and the sinner. I am the lover and the very love itself. I am the saint, the adorer, the worshipper and the follower. I am God.

THE SEARCH

I

I have been a wanderer long
In this world of transient things.
I have known the passing pleasures thereof.
As the rainbow is beautiful,
But soon vanishes into nothingness,
So have I known,
From the very foundation of the world,
The passing away of all things
Beautiful, joyous and pleasurable.

In search of the Eternal
I lost myself in the fleeting.
All things have I tasted in search of Truth.

In bygone ages
Have I known
The pleasures of the transient world—
The tender mother with her children,
The arrogant and the free,
The beggar that wanders the face of the earth,
The contentment of the wealthy,
The woman of enticements,
The beautiful and the ugly,

The man of authority, the man of power,
The man of consequence, the bestower and the guardian,
The oppressed and the oppressor,
The liberator and the tyrant,
The man of great possessions,
The man of renunciation, the sannyasi,
The man of activity and the man of dreams,
The arrogant priest in gorgeous robes, and the humble worshipper,
The poet, the artist and the creator.

At all the altars of the world have I worshipped,
All religions have known me,
Many ceremonies have I performed,
In the pomp of the world have I rejoiced,
In the battles of defeat and victory have I fought,
The despiser and the despised,
The man acquainted with grief
And agonies of many sorrows,
The man of pleasure and abundance.

In the secret recesses of my heart have I danced,
Many births and deaths have I known,
In all these fleeting realms have I wandered,
In passing ecstasies, certain of their endurance,
And yet I never found that eternal Kingdom of Happiness.
Once
I sought for Thee—
The imperishable Truth,
The eternal Happiness,
The culmination of all Wisdom—
On the mountain top,
In the star-lit sky,
In the shadows of the soft moon,
In the temples of man,
In the books of the learned,
In the soft spring leaf,
In the dancing waters,
On the face of man,
In the bubbling brook,

In sorrow, in pain,
In joy and ecstasy—
I did not find Thee.

As the mountaineer that climbs great heights,
Leaving his many burdens at each step,
So have I climbed,
Throwing aside all transient things.

As the sannyasi with his robes of gold,
With the begging bowl of happiness,
So have I renounced.

As the gardener who kills
The destructive weed of the garden,
So have I annihilated the self.

As the winds,
So am I free and untrammeled.

Fresh and eager as the wind
That seeketh the hidden places of the valley,
So have I sought
The secret abodes of my soul
And purged myself of all things,
Past and present.

As, suddenly, the robes of silence
Fall over the noisy world,
So, instantly, have I found Thee
Deep in the heart of all things and in mine own.

On the mountain path
I sat on a rock,
And Thou wert beside me and in me,
All things being in Thee and in me.
Happy is the man that findeth Thee and me
In all things.

In the light of the setting sun,
Through the delicate lace of a spring tree,
I beheld Thee.

In the twinkling stars
I beheld Thee.
In the swift passing bird,
Disappearing into the black mountain,
I beheld Thee.

Thy glory has awakened the glory in me.

As I have found, O world,
The Truth, the eternal Happiness,
So do I desire to give.

Come, let us consider together,
Ponder together and be happy together;
Let us reason together and bring forth Happiness.

As I have tasted
And know full well the sorrows and pains,
The ecstasies and joys
Of this fleeting world,
So do I know your travail.
The glory of a butterfly passeth in a day,
So, O world, are thy delights and pleasures.
As the sorrows of a child,
So, O world, are thy sorrows and pains,
Many pleasures leading to many sorrows,
Many sorrows to greater sorrows,
Continual strife and ceaseless small victories.
As the delicate bud, suffering the long winter,
Blossoms forth and gives delicious scent to the air,
And withers away before the setting of the sun,
So are thy struggles, thy achievements, and thy death—
A wheel of pain and pleasure,
Birth and death.

As I lost myself in the transient things
In search of that eternal Happiness,
So, O world, art thou lost in the fleeting.
Awake and gather thy strength,
Look about and consider.

That unfading Happiness—
The Happiness that is the only Truth,
The Happiness that is the end of all search,
The Happiness that is the end of all questionings and doubt,
The Happiness that brings freedom from birth and death,
The Happiness that is the only law,
The Happiness that is the only refuge,
The Happiness that is the source of all things,
The Happiness that gives eternal comfort,
That true Happiness that is enlightenment—
Abides within thee.

As I have gained strength,
So would I give
This Happiness.
As I have gained affectionate detachment,
So would I give
This Happiness.
As I have gained passionate dispassion,
So would I give
This Happiness.
As I have conquered life and death,
So would I give
This Happiness.

Throw aside, O world, thy vanities
And follow me,
For I know the way up the mountain,
For I know the way through this turmoil and grief.

There is only
One Truth,
One Law,
One Refuge,
One Guide,
To this eternal Happiness.

Awake, arise,
Consider and gather thy strength.

II

As it is but for a night
The birds rest on a tree,
So have I communed with strangers,
In my long journey
Through many lands.

Out of every sheaf of corn
I drew a blade.

Out of every day
I gathered some advantage.

From the full-laden tree
I plucked a ripe fruit.

My days are swifter
Than the weaver's shuttle.

III

As one beholds through a small window
A single green leaf, a small patch of the vast blue sky,
So I began to perceive Thee,
In the beginning of all things.
As the leaf faded and withered, the patch covered as with dark
    cloud,
So didst Thou fade and vanish,
But to be reborn again,
As the single green leaf, as the small patch of the blue sky.

For many lives have I seen
The bleak winter and the green spring.
Prisoned in my little room,
I could not behold the entire tree nor the whole sky.
I swore there was no tree, nor the vast sky—
That was the Truth.

Through time and destruction
My window grew large.
I beheld
Now,
A branch with many leaves,
And a greater patch of the blue with many clouds.

I forgot the single green leaf, the small patch of the vast blue.
I swore there was no tree, nor the immense sky—
That was the Truth.

Weary of this prison,
This small cell,
I raged at my window.
With bleeding fingers
I tore away brick after brick,
I beheld,
Now,
The entire tree, its great trunk,
Its many branches, its thousand leaves,
And an immense part of the sky.
I swore there was no other tree, no other part to the sky—
That was the Truth.

This prison no longer holds me,
I flew away through the window.
O friend,
I behold every tree and the vast expanse of the limitless sky.
Though I live in every single leaf and in every small patch of the
    vast blue sky,
Though I live in every prison, looking out through every small
    casement—
Liberated am I.
Lo! not a thing shall bind me—
This is the Truth.

IV

O world,
Thou art seeking everywhere for Happiness.

In every clime,
Among all peoples,
Among the animals and among the green trees,
Beside the dancing waters,
Upon the stately mountains,
Amid the cool valleys,
And in the sun-parched lands,
Under the serene star-lit skies,
In the radiance of the setting sun,
In the freshness of the dawn—
All beings are searching for this Happiness.

Though thy sons build impenetrable walls
Around their country,
Shutting out the happiness they seek,
Though thy learned priests fight for the Gods they shall worship,
Though the contentment of the wealthy be stagnating,
Though the oppressed and the exploited be suffering,
Though the man of thought has not found the eternal solution,
Though the sannyasi, who renounces the world, has not gained
    enlightenment,
Though the beggar, that wanders from house to house for kindness
    has not found shelter,
Though thy people prefer the darkness of the night to the light of
    day,
Though thy people turn night into day—
All are searching for that lasting Happiness.

As the dreary tree longingly suffers for the spring and green
    happiness,
So all thy people look for that lasting Happiness.

The lady of fashion who depends on clothes and wealth,
The woman who is painted,
The girl who flirts,
The man who seeks happiness in clothes,
The man who drinks incessantly,
The man who cannot be happy unless playing at something,
The man who kills to enjoy,
The priest in his gorgeous robes,
The recluse with the loin cloth,
The actor dressed to please the audience,
The artist struggling to create,
The poet who pours into words the immensity of his thoughts and
    dreams,
The musician whose soul is thrilled with sound,
The saint in his asceticism,
The sinner, if there be one, who does not care for God or man,
The bourgeois who is frightened of all things—
All these are searching for happiness.

They buy and they sell,
They build magnificent palaces,
Surrounding themselves with all the beauty
That money can buy,
They plant gardens, the exquisite delight of the refined,
They cover themselves with jewels,
They quarrel and they are charming,
They drink without restraint,
They eat without restraint,
They are virulent and pacific,
They worship and curse,
They love and hate,
They die and are born again,
They are cruel to man and beast,
They destroy and create,
They produce and annihilate—
Yet they are all seeking happiness,
Happiness in transient things.

The rose, beautiful and glorious,
Dieth tomorrow.

In search of happiness
They build vast structures,
Call them Churches,
And enter therein,
But it eludes them, as in the naked streets.
They invent a God to satisfy themselves,
But they never find in Him what they long for.

The incense, the flowers, the candles,
The gorgeous robes, the thrilling music,
Are but enticements for that search.
The deep note of the distant bell,
The monotonous prayer,
Calling, crying and begging,
Are but the gropings in the dark
For that lasting Happiness.

In search of happiness
They build cool, gigantic Temples,
The product of many minds,
The work of many hands;
The chantings, the smoke of the camphor,
The beauty of the sacred lotus,
Do not satisfy their craving.

In search of happiness
They bribe, they corrupt, they make unholy
The earth, the seas and mountains.
Their graven images do not answer their call.
As the mountain stream sweeps all things before it,
So is their structure of happiness destroyed in an instant;
They destroy each other in their jealous love.

In search of happiness
They give labels, pretty-sounding names
To each other,
And think they have found

The source of Eternity,
Solved the problem of their sorrow.

In search of happiness
They marry, rejoicing in their new-found happiness;
They are happy as the flower
That blossoms with the sun
And dies with the sun.
They change their love and renew their rejoicings.
They are full and bubbling over
With ecstasy,
And, in an instant,
Sorrow is the outcome of their fleeting joy.

As the cloud, fully laden, that empties itself
And vanishes from the heavens,
Leaving again the barren sky,
So is their love, that is full,
That is powerful, that creates and destroys.
Their love, so triumphant in the beginning,
So strong with desires,
So beautiful in the full bloom,
So unrestrained in its fulfillment,
Fades as the leaf.
To be born again,
Fading again as the leaf.
As the sorrowing tree
That has lost its happy leaves,
So is the man
Who sought happiness
Through love.

In solitude,
In crowded streets,
They search for happiness,
All the world moans for happiness.
The winds whisper,
The storms threaten,
But the man looks for happiness

In the passing things,
In the transient things,
In the things that he can touch and perceive,
And groans after the loss of his happiness,
As the child that cries
After the broken doll.

For their happiness fades and withers
As the tender leaf.

Search their hopes,
Their longings,
Their desires,
Their selfishness,
Their quarrels and angers,
Their dignities,
Their ambitions,
Their glories,
Their rewards,
Their distinctions—
There is disillusionment,
There is vanity,
There is unhappiness.

Search their class distinctions,
Their spiritual distinctions,
Their limitations,
Their openness,
Their prejudices,
Their embraces—
There is an uncertainty of purpose,
There is an uncertainty of happiness.

Wherever you may look,
Wherever you may wander,
In whatever clime you may abide,
There is sorrow, there is pain,
Unsatisfiable voids,
Open aching wounds, bared and exposed,
Or covered over

With the panoply of great rejoicing.
No man sayeth—"My happiness is indestructible."
There is everywhere decay and death,
And the renewal of life.

So are they that seek happiness in the passing—
Their happiness is of the moment.
As the butterfly, that tasteth the honey of every flower,
That dieth in the day,
As the desert that is deluged with the rain
Yet remaineth a weary land without a shadow—
So is their happiness
As the sands of the sea are their actions
In search of this happiness.
As the aged and mighty tree
That towers into the sky
And is felled by the axe in a moment—
So is their happiness.

They look to their happiness
In the transient,
In the fleeting,
In the objective,
And they find it not.
Such is their fleeting and unsatisfied happiness.

Can you grow the tree of Happiness on sand?

The Happiness that will not fade by usage,
That increases by action,
That increases by feeling,
That is born of Truth,
That never decays,
That knows no beginning, no end,
That is free,
The Happiness that is Eternal,
They have never tasted.

The Happiness that knows
Of no loneliness,
Of immense certainty,

Of detachment,
Of love that is free of persons,
That is free from prejudices,
That is not bound by tradition,
That is not bound by authority,
That is not bound by superstitions,
That is of no religion.
The Happiness
That is not at the command of another,
That is of no priest,
That is of no sect,
That requires no labels,
That is bound by no law,
That cannot be shaken by God or man,
That is solitary and embraces all,
That blows from the snow-clad mountains
That blows from the hot desert,
That burns,
That heals,
That destroys,
That creates,
That delights in solitude and in numbers,
That fills the soul through Eternity.
That is the God,
The wife, the mother,
The husband, the father,
And the child.
That is of no class,
That is of the aristocracy of divinity,
That is the refinement of the refined,
That is a philosophy unto itself.
That is as vast as the seas,
That is open as the skies,
That is profound as the lake,
That is tranquil as the peaceful valley,
That is serene as the mountain,
That is beyond the shadow of death,
That is beyond the limitations of birth,

That is as the strength of the hills,
That bears the fruit of many generations,
That is the consummation of all desire,
That is the ecstasy of purpose,
That is the source of all existence,
That is the well whose waters feed the worlds,
That is the ecstasy, the joy,
That is the dancing star of our being,
That giveth divine discontentment,
That is born of Eternity,
That is the destruction of self,
That is the pool of wisdom,
That creates happiness in others
That has dominion over all things—
Such happiness thou hast never tasted,
O world.

For thou hast been fed on the food of another,
Thou hast been taught by the lips of another,
Thou hast been taught to draw thy strength from another,
Thou hast been taught that thy happiness lies in another,
That thy redemption is at the hands of another,
That wisdom is in the mouth of another,
That Truth can only be attained through another,
Thou hast been taught to worship the God of another,
To adore at the altar of another,
To discipline thyself to the authority of another,
To shape thyself in the mold of another,
To abide in the shadow of another,
To grow in the protection of another,
Thou hast been taught to lay thy foundations in another,
To hear with the ears of another,
To feel with the heart of another,
To think with the mind of another;
Thou hast been fed with the enticements of transient things,
Thou hast been fed with the food that never satisfies,
Thou hast been fed with the knowledge that disappears with strife.

Thou hast been fed at the hands of the satisfied,
With the false and the fleeting.

Thou hast been nourished by laws, by governments, by
    philosophies,
Thou hast been led, driven and exposed,
Thou hast been sheltered under the shadow
That changes from moment to moment,
Thou hast been nurtured by false truths and false gods,
Thou hast been stimulated by false desires,
Thou hast been fed on false ambitions,
Thou hast been fed with the fruits of the earth,
O world.

Thou hast been taught to seek Truth in the fleeting,
Thou hast been nourished by the transient things,
In these thou shalt never find that Happiness
For which thy soul doth seek and suffer.

But,
As the diver plunges deep into the sea
For the pearl,
Risking his life in search of the transient,
So must thou plunge deep down within thyself
In search of Eternity.
As the adventurous mountaineer that climbs to conquer,
So must thou climb to that intoxicating height,
Where thou seest all things in their true proportion.
As the lotus that pushes heavenward through mire,
So must thou push aside all transient things
If thou wouldst discover that Kingdom of Happiness.
As the majestic tree depends for its strength on its hidden roots,
And plays with the great passing winds,
So must thou establish thy hidden strength deep within thyself,
And play with the passing world.
As the swift-running river knows its source,
So must thou know thine own being.
As the soft blue lake whose depth no man knows,

So must thy depth be unfathomable.
As the seas contain a multitude of living things,
So in thee are there hidden secrets of the worlds.
As on the mountain side, at various altitudes, different flowers grow,
So in thee are there degrees of beauty.
As the earth is full of hidden treasures which no man hath seen,
So in thee are hidden secrets, unknown to thyself.

As the winds possess immense, inexhaustible power,
So in thee lieth great unconquerable energy.
As the mountain-tops dance in the light of the sun,
So shalt thou dance in the light of thy knowledge.
As there is an ever-changing vision on the winding mountain path,
So in thee there is a constant unfoldment.
As the distant star that scintillates of a dark night,
So is he that hath discovered himself.

In thee alone is the God, for there is no other God,
Thou art the God that all religions and nations worship,
In thee alone are joy, ecstasy, power and strength,
In thee alone is the power to grow, to change and alter,
In thee alone are the experiences of many ages gathered,
In thee alone is the source of all things—
Love, hate, jealousy, fear, anger and sweetness—
In thee alone lies the power to create or to destroy,
In thee alone is the beginning of all thought, feeling and action,
In thee alone lies nobility,
In thee alone is no loneliness.

Thou art the master of all things.
Thou art the source of all things.

In thee alone lies the power to do good and to do evil,
In thee alone lies the power to create Heaven and Hell,
In thee alone lies the power to control the future and the present.
Thou art the master of Time,
In thee alone is the Kingdom of Happiness,
In thee alone is the eternal Truth,
In thee alone is the well of inexhaustible Love.

O world,
If thou wouldst know all the hidden secrets,
The treasures of many ages,
The experiences of many centuries,
The accumulation of power of many generations,
The thought of the past,
The ecstasies, joys, sorrow and pain of bygone ages,
And the great and foolish actions of the many lives that lie behind
    thee,
The centuries of uncertainty and doubt,
If thou wouldst know of the immense future,
Of the great heights of joyous growth,
Of the adventure of good and evil,
Of the result of all thought, of all feelings, and of all actions,
Of the many past lives and of the many future lives,
If thou wouldst know of thy hates, of thy jealousies,
Of thine agonies, of thy pleasures and pains,
Of thine ecstatic love, of thy joyous rapture,
Of thy burning devotion, of thy bubbling enthusiasm,
Of thy joyous seriousness, of thine aching worship,
Of thine unrestrained adoration,
If thou wouldst concern thyself with the lasting,
With the eternal, with the indestructible,
With divinity, with immortality,
With wisdom which is the pool of Heaven,
If thou wouldst know of that everlasting Kingdom of Happiness,
If thou wouldst know of that beauty that never fades or decays,
If thou wouldst know of that truth that is imperishable and alone—
Then, O world,
Look deep within thyself
With eyes clear, if thou wouldst perceive all things.

As the tranquil pool that reflects the heavens above,
So shall all things find their reflection in thee.
As the flower that blossoms forth in the warm sunshine,
So must thou unfold if thou wouldst know thyself.
As the eagle soars into the heavens, unrestrained and free,

So must thou soar if thou wouldst know thyself.
As the river that dances down to the sea,
So must thou dance if thou wouldst know thyself.
As the mountain is strong and full of power,
So must thou be if thou wouldst know thyself.
As the precious stone sparkles in the sun,
So must thou shine if thou wouldst know thyself.
As the mother is to the babe, tender with affection,
So must thou be if thou wouldst know thyself.
As the winds are free and untrammeled,
So must thou be if thou wouldst know thyself.

If thou wouldst taste of all these things,
O world,
And walk with me in the Kingdom of Happiness,
Thou must be free from that poison of Truth—
Prejudice—
For thou art immense in thy prejudice,
Both the ancient and the inexperienced.
Thou must be free from that narrowness of tradition,
The narrowness of custom, habit, feeling and thought,
The narrowness of religion, worship and adoration,
The narrowness of nation,
The narrowness of family and of possession,
The narrowness of love,
The narrowness of friendship,
The narrowness of thy God and of thy form of approach to Him,
The narrowness of thy conception of beauty,
The narrowness of thy work and of thy duty,
The narrowness of thine achievements and glories,
The narrowness of thy rewards and chastisements,
The narrowness of thy desires, ambitions and purpose,
The narrowness of thy longings and satisfactions,
The narrowness of thy discontentments and contentments,
The narrowness of thy struggles and victories,
The narrowness of thine ignorance and knowledge,
The narrowness of thy teachings and laws,

The narrowness of thine ideas and views—
Thou must be free from all these.

Prejudice is as a shadow
On the face of the mountain,
As a dark cloud
In the fair skies,
As the withered rose
That ceases to delight the world,
As the blight that destroys
The bloom of a ripe fruit,
As the bird that has lost
The power of its wings,
As the man that hath no ears,
Deaf to sweet music,
As the man that hath no eyes,
Blind to the gorgeous sunset,
As the delights of experience
To the man that is enfeebled.

Prejudice is as the agitated lake
That cannot reflect the beauty of the skies,
As a barren rock of the mountain,
As the weary land of a shadowless country,
As the dry bed of the river
That knows not the delights
Of the waters of many summers,
As the tree that has lost its green happiness,
As the woman that is childless,
As the breath of winter
That withereth all things,
As the shadow of death
In a happy land.

Prejudice is evil,
It is a corrupter of the world,
It is a destroyer of the beautiful,
It is the root of all sorrow,

It has its being in ignorance,
It is a state of utter darkness where light cannot find its way,
It is an abomination,
A sin against Truth.

If thou wouldst know thyself,
Thou must cut thyself free from this weed that binds thee,
That suffocates thee,
That destroys thy vision,
That kills thine affection,
That prevents thy thought.

When thou art free, untrammeled,
When thy body is controlled and relaxed,
When thine eyes can perceive all things in their pure nakedness,
When thy heart is serene and burdened with affection,
When thy mind is well poised,
Then, O world,
The gates of that Garden,
The Kingdom of Happiness,
Are open.

V

From the ancient of times,
From the very foundation of the earth,
The end for all things
Have I known.

As the mighty river knows
At the very beginning of its birth
The end of its long journey,
Though it wander through many lands,
So have I known.

As in the time of winter
The barren tree
Knows the coming joys of the spring,
So have I known.

Long have I wandered
Through many lives,
In many lands,
Amidst many peoples,
In search of this end
I have known.

As the stagnant pools that are purified
With the coming rains,
So had I remained
Motionless,
Till the hurricane of sorrow
Cleansed me.

Burdened have I been
With many possessions,
With the wealth of the world,
With the comforts that bring stagnation.

Rejoiced have I been
In the satisfaction of a multitude of things,
Till the storm of tears
Washed away the pride of abundance.
And as the lands of the desert
Are without shadows,
So had my life become.

I worshipped at the altars
Of way-side shrines,
Whose Gods have denied me
Of the end that I have known.

Their priests held me
In thrall
By the magic of their words,
By the intoxication of their incense.
In the sheltering shadows of the temple walls
I remained, in darkness
Weeping for the end I have known.
Till anew
The whirlwind of pain

Threw me out again
On the open road.

I created philosophies, and creeds,
Complicated theories of life;
I buried myself
In the intellectual creations of man,
Great in the arrogance thereof.
As of a sudden
The storm breaks,
So was I left naked,
Overwhelmed by the agony
Of the transient things.

Great was my love,
Immense was the satisfaction thereof.
I sang,
I danced
In the ecstasy of my love,
But as fades the tender rose
In the full days of summer,
So my love withered
In the full days of my enjoyment.
I was as empty as the wide skies,
I wept for the end
I have known.

Renouncing all,
As naked as I came,
I withdrew from the world of pleasure,
In solitude,
Under the great trees,
In seclusion
Of the peaceful valley,
I sought for the end
That my soul cried for,
The end that I have known
Through the ages of time.

As the flower sleeps of a night,
Withholding its glory
For the joys of the morrow,
So, gathering my strength,
I delved deep
Into the secret stores of my heart
For the joy of discovery.
As one beholds the light
At the end of a dark passage,
So I beheld
The end of my search,
The end I have known.

As the builder
Lays brick upon brick,
For the edifice of his desire,
So, from the ancient of times,
From the very foundation of the earth,
Have I gathered,
The dust of experience,
Life after life,
For the consummation
Of my heart's desire.

Behold!
My house is complete and full,
And now I am free to depart.

As the mighty river knows
At the very beginning of its birth
The end of its long journey,
So have I known.

As in the time of winter
The barren tree
Knows the coming joys of the spring,
So have I known.

From the ancient of times,
From the very foundation of the earth,

The end for all things
Have I known.

Lo! the hour has come,
The hour that I have known.
Liberated am I,
Free from life and death,
Sorrow and pleasure call me no more,
Detached am I in affection,
Beyond the dreams of the Gods am I.

As the moon is full and serene
In the days of harvest,
So am I
In the days of my Liberation.
Simple as the tender leaf am I,
For in me are many winters and many springs.

As the dewdrop is of the sea,
So am I born
In the ocean of liberation.

As the mysterious river
Enters the open seas,
So have I entered
Into the world of Liberation.

This is the end I have known.

THE
IMMORTAL FRIEND

Wherever I look, Thou art there.
I am full of Thy glory.
I am burning with Thy happiness.
I weep for all men
That do not behold Thee.
In what manner
Shall I show them
Thy glory?

I sat a-dreaming in a room of great silence.
The early morning was still and breathless,
The great blue mountains stood against the dark skies, cold and
    clear,
Round the dark log house
The black and yellow birds were welcoming the sun.

I sat on the floor, with legs crossed, meditating,
Forgetting the sunlit mountains,
The birds,
The immense silence,
And the golden sun.

I lost the feel of my body,
My limbs were motionless,

Relaxed and at peace.
A great joy of unfathomable depth filled my heart.
Eager and keen was my mind, concentrated.
Lost to the transient world,
I was full of strength.

As the Eastern breeze
That suddenly springs into being
And calms the weary world,
There in front of me
Seated cross-legged,
As the world knows Him
In His yellow robes, simple and magnificent,
Was the Teacher of Teachers.

Looking at me,
Motionless the Mighty Being sat.
I looked and bowed my head,
My body bent forward of itself.

That one look
Showed the progress of the world,
Showed the immense distance between the world
And the greatest of its Teachers.
How little it understood,
And how much He gave.
How joyously He soared,
Escaping from birth and death,
From its tyranny and entangling wheel.

Enlightenment attained,
He gave to the world, as the flower gives
Its scent,
The Truth.

As I looked at the sacred feet
That once trod the happy
Dust of India,
My heart poured forth its devotion,
Limitless and unfathomable,
Without restraint and without effort.

I lost myself in that happiness.
My mind so easily and strangely
Understood the Truth
He longed for and attained.
I lost myself in that happiness.
My soul grasped the infinite simplicity
Of Truth.
I lost myself in that happiness.

Thou art the Truth,
Thou art the Law,
Thou art the Refuge,
Thou art the Guide,
The Companion and the Beloved.
Thou hast ravished my heart,
Thou hast conquered my soul,
In Thee have I found my comfort,
In Thee is my truth established.

Where Thou hast trodden,
Do I follow.
Where Thou hast suffered and conquered,
Do I gather strength.
Where Thou hast renounced,
Do I grow,
Dispassionate, detached.

Like the stars
Have I become.
Happy is he that knoweth Thee
Eternally.

Like the sea, unfathomable
Is my love.
The Truth have I attained,
And calm grows my spirit.

But yesterday
I longed to withdraw
From the aching world
Into some secluded mountain spot,

Untrammeled,
Free,
Away from all things,
In search of Thee.
And now Thou hast appeared
Unto me.

I carry Thee in my heart.
Look where I may, Thou art there,
Calm, happy,
Filling my world—
The embodiment of Truth.

My heart is strong,
My mind is concentrated,
I am full of Thee.
As the Eastern breeze
That suddenly springs into being,
And calms the weary world,
So have I realized.

I am the Truth,
I am the Law,
I am the Refuge,
I am the Guide,
The Companion and the Beloved.

II

Look where I may, Thou art there,
Calm, happy,
Filling my world—
The embodiment of Truth.

As one beholds a light
In the dark
At a distance,
I saw Thee.

I have walked towards Thee
Through many lives—
In sorrow, in joy,
In doubt, in suspicion,
Over thorns, over fair fields,
On the pavements of crowded cities.

I have known
From the very foundation of the earth
Of Thy glory,
Of Thine existence,
Of Thy beauty, that thrilled my soul.
Never was I certain,
Never was I allowed to be at peace
With myself,
With man,
Or with the fair heavens.
Out of the great uncertainty,
Certainty was born.

Like the Eastern breeze
That suddenly springs into being
And calms the weary world,
So have I realized.
I walk henceforth in Thy shadow.

Because Thou art my eternal Companion,
I am strong—
Strong as the stream
That rushes down the mountain side.
Because Thou art my counselor,
I am unshakable,
Because of Thee,
I am full of wisdom,
Because Thou hast sent me out,
I am as nothing, as the passing wind,
But because Thou hast shown Thyself to me,
I am as the rivers

That dance down to the sea.
Because of Thy bidding,
Whatever I do is for Thee.
My heart is aflame,
For I have come near unto Thee
Everlastingly.

Each breath is transforming me
Into Thine image.

Because Thou hast given me,
I am full,
Full as the ocean,
Though all the rivers
Do flow into it.

Thy majesty has awakened
The power in me
To shout from the mountain tops
Thy truth.

Thy look
Has burnt away
The dross.
I am pure.
I am holy.

What the rose is to the rose petal,
So art Thou to me.
As the mountain top
That disappears into the clouds,
So my love for Thee
Disappears
Into space.

As on the sunlit sea the waters dance,
Joyous in their ecstasy,
So is my heart
Dancing for love of Thee.
As the small raindrop
Mingles in the vast ocean,

So have I lost
Myself
In Thee.

As the shadows
Grow of an evening,
So has my soul
Grown immense
In Thy Light.

My love for Thee
Has awakened the love
For all.
I must bring the world
To Thee.
I must make Thee
Their eternal Companion.
They must know Thee
As I know Thee—
The perfect,
The simple,
The glorified,
The Fountain of Truth.

Knowing Thee,
They will set aside their toys,
Their small worlds, their playthings,
Their pomp,
The entanglements
Of their religions,
Their rites,
Their ceremonies.

What is religion?
What is worship?
What are the temples
And altars
Of the world?

Thou art the end
Of all sorrow,

Of all joy,
Of all knowledge,
Of all search.

Thou art the goal of all things.
In Thee alone lies
Enlightenment—
The Happiness of the world.

Look where I may, Thou art there,
Calm, happy,
Filling my world—
The embodiment of Truth.

I am the Truth,
I am the Law,
I am the Refuge,
I am the Guide, the Companion and the Beloved.

III

Through the austere dignity of the yellow robe
Thou wert born unto me.
Through the certainty of knowledge
Thou hast appeared unto me.
Through the immensity of happiness
Thou hast shown Thyself unto me.
Through the great silence of the morning
Thou hast created the universe unto me.
Through the sunlight of the world
Thou hast carried me to the mountain top.

And unto me Thou wert born.

Over Thy head was the flame
That burns away all sorrow,
All pain, all anxiety.
Thy face was like unto the rose petal,
Perfect, soft, lovely,
Youthful with the age of many centuries.

In Thy face I beheld my own face.
In Thine eyes was the laughter of Youth,
The delight of the Spring,
The joyous merriment of the world.

The music of Thy flute
Hath ravished my heart.
There is born in me
A new tender merriment.
The sea of many waters
Hath entered into my heart:
The bubbling brook,
The boisterous storm,
The angry waters,
The pleasant breeze.

I smell the flowers at Thy feet,
I behold the lane
Where walks the world,
The dust, the cow,
And the cow-herd.

The scent of the sacred flower fills the air,
I hear the temple bells,
And the laughter of the world.

The jewels of the world
Are in Thine eyes.

The world weeps for Thee
In their wild and merry dancing.

O Love, with the flute,
Thou art myself.

O Beloved,
Thou art the ecstasy of my soul.

I have found Thee
Through the happiness of many lives.

O world,
In thee I behold the face of my Beloved.

IV

He walked towards me and I stood still.
My heart and soul gathered strength.
The trees and the birds listened with unexpected silence.
There was thunder in the skies—
Then, utter peace.

I saw Him look at me,
And my vision became vast.
My eyes saw and my mind understood.
My heart embraced all things,
For a new love was born unto me.

A new glory thrilled my being,
For He walked before me, and I followed, my head high.
The tall trees I saw through Him,
Gently waving in welcome,
The dead leaf, the mud,
The sparkling water and the withered branches.
The heavily laden and chattering villagers
Walked through Him—ignorant and laughing,
The barking dogs rushed, through Him, at me.
A barrack of a house became an enchanted abode,
Its red roof melting into the setting sun.
The garden was a fairy land,
The flowers were the fairies.

Standing against the dark evening sky,
I saw Him
In His eternal glory.

He walked before me
Down the little narrow path,
Always looking, while I followed.

He was at the door of my room,
I passed through Him.

Purified, with a new song in my heart,
I remain.

He is before me forever.
Look where I may, He is there.
I see all things through Him.
His glory has filled me and awakened a glory that I have never
    known.

An eternal peace is my vision,
Glorifying all things.
He is ever before me.

V

The sun was setting
As I stood on a hill-top,
Watching it disappear
Behind the mountains.

In the midst of that radiance,
Clad in a cloud of yellow,
Thou wert seated.

The whole vast heaven
Paused in adoration.
The sky, the clouds,
In robes of yellow,
Were Thy worshippers,
Thy disciples.

The mortal world
Joined in Thine adoration,
Shouting with joy—
The birds,
The distant valley,
The passing vehicles
Far away,
The cricket,
The grasshopper,

The wind
And the trees.

The black mountains
Stood amazed
In their dance,
Fearing their own
Mighty sight.

Then utter silence—
All things perceiving Thee
As Thou art.

In that great silence
An immense desire
Was born in me
To bring the world to Thee,
To Thy perfection
And to Thy happiness.

Thou art the only altar,
Though men worship
At the altars
Of many temples.
Thine is the only
Imperishable Truth,
Though men clothe it
By many names.

I love the world,
And all the things thereof.
I will bring the world
To adore Thee,
To worship Thee;
For Thy beauty
Is truth.

Immense happiness
Fills my being,
For I have found
Thee.

Thou shalt not disappear
Though a thousand suns
Shall set over the mountain.

As the sunset
Grows more splendid
From moment to moment,
Changing constantly,
So my desire
For Thee
Grows
More glorious,
More perfect.
It shall fill
The heart of all men,
Till Thy perfection
Be perceived.

In Thine eye
Is the whirlwind,
The soft breeze,
The sacred Himavat,
The low plain,
The happy valley,
And the blue skies—
All things are in Thee.

Thou art the happiness
Of the world.
The Path of Happiness
Is the Path of Truth.

VI

O listen!
I shall sing to thee the song of my Beloved.

Where the soft green slopes of the still mountains
Meet the blue shimmering waters of the noisy sea,

Where the bubbling brook shouts in ecstasy,
Where the still pools reflect the calm heavens,
There thou wilt meet with my Beloved.

In the vale where the cloud hangs in loneliness,
Searching the mountain for rest,
In the still smoke climbing heavenwards,
In the hamlet towards the setting sun,
In the thin wreaths of the fast disappearing clouds,
There thou wilt meet with my Beloved.

Among the dancing tops of the tall cypress,
Among the gnarled trees of great age,
Among the frightened bushes that cling to the earth,
Among the long creepers that hang lazily,
There thou wilt meet with my Beloved.

In the plowed fields where noisy birds are feeding,
On the shaded path that winds along the full, motionless river,
Beside the banks where the waters lap,
Amidst the tall poplars that play ceaselessly with the winds,
In the dead tree of last summer's lightning,
There thou wilt meet with my Beloved.

In the still blue skies
Where heaven and earth meet,
In the breathless air,
In the morn burdened with incense,
Among the rich shadows of a noon-day,
Among the long shadows of an evening,
Amidst the gay and radiant clouds of the setting sun,
On the path on the waters at the close of the day,
There thou wilt meet with my Beloved.

In the shadows of the stars,
In the deep tranquillity of dark nights,
In the reflection of the moon on still waters,
In the great silence before the dawn,
Among the whispering of waking trees,
In the cry of the bird at morn,
Amidst the wakening of shadows,

Amidst the sunlit tops of the far mountains,
In the sleepy face of the world,
There thou wilt meet with my Beloved.

Keep still, O dancing waters,
And listen to the voice of my Beloved.

In the happy laughter of children
Thou canst hear Him.
The music of the flute
Is His voice.
The startled cry of a lonely bird
Moves thy heart to tears,
For thou hearest His voice.
The roar of the age-old sea
Awakens the memories
That have been lulled to sleep
By His voice.
The soft breeze that stirs
The treetops lazily,
Brings to thee the sound
Of His voice.

The thunder among the mountains
Fills thy soul
With the strength
Of His voice.
In the roar of a vast city,
Through the shrill moan of swift passing vehicles,
In the throb of a distant engine,
Through the voices of the night,
The cry of sorrow,
The shout of joy,
Through the ugliness of anger,
Comes the voice of my Beloved.

In the distant blue isles,
On the soft dewdrop,
On the breaking wave,
On the sheen of waters,

On the wing of the flying bird,
On the tender leaf of spring,
Thou wilt see the face of my Beloved.

In the sacred temple,
In the halls of dancing,
On the holy face of the sannyasi,
In the lurches of the drunkard,
With the harlot and with the chaste,
Thou wilt meet with my Beloved.

On the fields of flowers,
In the towns of squalor and dirt,
With the pure and the unholy,
In the flower that hides divinity,
There is my well-Beloved.

Oh! the sea
Has entered my heart.
In a day,
I am living a hundred summers.
O friend,
I behold my face in thee,
The face of my well-Beloved.

This is the song of my love.

VII

As the rain cleanses
The tree by the roadside,
So the dust of ages
Has been washed away in me.

As the tree sparkles
In the sun
After the soft rain,
So my soul delighteth
In Thee.

As the tree
Looketh to its roots
For its immense strength,
So do I look to Thee
Who art the root of my strength.

As the smoke mounteth heavenwards
In a straight column,
Of a still evening
So have I grown
Towards Thee.

As the little pool
On the road
Reflecteth the face of heaven,
So my heart
Reflecteth Thy happiness.

As the solitary cloud
That hangs over the mountain
The envy of the valley,
So have I hung,
For generation after generation,
In a lonely place.

As the great cloud
That hasteneth
Before the mighty wind,
So descend I
Into the valley.
Into the valley
Where there is sorrow
And transient happiness,
Where there is birth and death,
Where there is shadow and light,
Where there is strife and a passing peace,
Where there is comfort of stagnation,
Where to think is to grieve,
Where to feel is to create sorrow.

Into that valley
I shall descend,
For I have conquered,
For in me
Thou art born.

As the light pierces through darkness,
So Thy truth
Shall pierce the world.
As the rain purifieth the earth
And cleanseth all things thereof,
So shall I cleanse the world
With Thy truth.
For many ages,
Through many lives,
Have I prepared,
But now,
Behold, the cup is full.

The world shall drink of it.
Man shall grow
Into Thy divinity.
Thy happiness shall shine
On his face.
For Thy messenger
Shall go forth.

I am he
That openeth the heart of man,
That giveth comfort.

I am the Truth,
I am the Law,
I am the Refuge,
I am the Guide, the Companion and the Beloved.

VIII

O friend,
Tell me of God.

Where is He, by what manner do I find Him,
Among what climes, in what abodes?
Tell me, I am weary.

Read the Vedas,
Do tapas, meditate,
Perform rites and ceremonies,
Practice austerities and renounce,
Pray at His temple, among flowers and incense,
Bathe in the sacred rivers,
Visit the holy places,
Be a devotee and pure of intelligence,
In Kailas is His abode—
There you will find Him, cried many.

Obey the Law,
Take refuge in the Order,
Kill not, steal not and commit no sin,
Go to the shrine,
Enter Nirvana—
There you will find Him, cried many.

Read the Holy Book,
Pray at His church—there be many—
This church will lead you to Him but beware of that.

Serve, sacrifice,
Do not judge, be merciful,
In Heaven is His throne—
There you will find Him, cried many.

Read the only Book
Of the only God,
Visit His abode on earth,
Pray at the mosque,
At the setting of the sun worship Him,
Bahisht is his abode—
There you will find Him, cried many.

Work, work for humanity,
Serve, serve your fellow-creatures,

Follow this but beware of that Path,
Do the will of God,
Follow blindly for I hold the key to His abode.
Grasp this opportunity He offers you,
Sorrow and happiness lead to Him,
If you do this, your search will end—
Then you will find Him, shouted many.

I am weary, tired by the passage of time.
Traveling on no path, I have come to Thee,
Thou hast revealed Thyself to me.

Oh! Thou art the round stone
That grinds the rice in the peaceful village
Amidst songs and laughter.
Thou art the graven image
That men worship in temples,
With chants and solemn music.
Thou art the dead leaf
That lies torn on the dusty road
Trodden by the weary traveler.
Thou art the solitary pine
That stands majestic
On the lonely hill.

Thou art the lame and mangy creature
That comes to my door with a haunted look, hungry,
That men abhor.
Thou art the mighty elephant
That is gaily robed,
Carrying the nobles of the land.
Thou art the naked beggar
That wanders from house to house
Wearily crying for alms.
Thou art the great of the land
That are rich in possessions and books,
That are well-fed and satisfied.
Thou art the priests of all temples
That are learned, proud and certain.

Thou art the harlot, the sinner, the saint and the heretic.

My search is at an end,
In Thee I behold all things.
I myself, am God.

IX

Telling of beads—they are but dead wood.
Bathing in holy rivers—they are but waters.
Worshipping at temples—they are but the walls of naked stone.
Writing of books—they are but flowers of words.
Thinkest thou, O friend, to juggle with Me?
As the lotus abides with the waters,
So do I live with thee, eternally.

Adorn Me with thy jewels,
Clothe Me with thy garments,
Feed Me with thy delicacies,
Flatter Me with thy glories.
Thinkest thou, O friend, to juggle with Me?
As the lotus abides with the waters,
So do I live with thee, eternally.

Search for thy happiness in passing things,
Pursue thy passionate trivialities,
Drink deep for thy oblivion,
Chase the butterfly from flower to flower.
Thinkest thou, O friend, to juggle with Me?
As the lotus abides with the waters,
So do I live with thee, eternally.

Rich is the shadow of a summer's day.

Our journey ends, O friend,
When thou and I meet.

X

As the delicate spire climbs eagerly into the blue skies,
O my Beloved, so my heart soars into space in search of Thee.
As the butterfly tastes the hidden honey of the fast-fading flower,
O my Beloved, so have I played with Thee among the manifested—
Changing, decaying.

By offerings, by alms and by the building of many a temple,
Have I sought to establish Thee.
As the sparkling dewdrop that hangs on the tree-tops
Above the world,
To fade in the morning sun,
So have my great foundations in the kingdoms of the manifest
Been destroyed.

As the stars of a night
About me are Thy creations.
By yoga, by austerities,
Life after life,
Have I chased Thee among the shadows of Thy manifestations.
Ever eluding, ever enticing, ever disappointing,
Have been my glimpses of Thee.

But, my Beloved, my eternal love,
O Thou, the desire of my heart,
I have found Thee, in the unmanifest,
In the indestructible.
As the rainbow vanishes near the green earth,
So has my search vanished among the flowers of Thy creation.

In me Thou art established,
Imperishable, ineffable, everlasting.
O Beloved,
Thou art established in the temple of my heart.

I am the Beloved, the desire of all hearts,
I am the Playmate in the shadow of creation.

XI

In the quiet evening
When the leaf is still,
When the flower is weary of the day
And the bud is rejoicing for the morrow,
When the shadows are long
And the smoke is mounting in a still column,
When the world is breathless,
Oh! with the lark I climbed
To the abode of my Beloved.

I have wandered far into the realms of the unreal
In search of the real.
Many births and many deaths have been my lot.
With the setting of a single day
Have I known many joys, many sorrows,
But Thou hast eluded me,
O Thou, the embodiment of Truth.

I have brought to Thee all my experience,
All my woes and my joys.
I have worshipped with folded hands in many a temple,
But at my eager approach faded the image of truth.

I have loved and the glories of the earth have delighted me.
I was full of knowledge, enjoying the admiration of the world.
I adorned myself with priestly robes,
But in silence the gods of my adoration looked down.

As the mountain is to the valley—distant, forbidding—
So hast Thou been to me.
Thou hast ever remained with Thy face turned.
Thou hast been as a star—far away, unreal.
Thou wert ever the image,
I ever the worshipper.
Not a man knew of Thine abode;
Thou wert ever far away, fantastical, mysterious.

Sometimes immense fear filled my heart,
Often great hopes,
At times complete indifference and weariness.
Without Thee, I was as an empty shell.

As the potter's wheel,
I went round and round,
Consumed by continual action.
I brought to Thee the flower of my heart,
The great delight of my mind,
But as the dead leaf in autumn,
I was torn and trodden down.

As the tree on the mountain
Grows in solitude and strength,
Likewise, life after life,
I grew in solitude and stature,
I reached the mountain top.

Till in the long last,
O Guru of Gurus,
I tore the veil that separated Thee from myself,
That veil that set Thee apart.

Now, my Beloved, Thou and I are one.
As the lotus makes the waters beautiful,
So Thou and I complete the perfection of Life.

O Guru,
Thy Play is my play,
Thy Love is my love.
Thy smile has filled my heart,
My work is Thy creation.
Thou hast bowed to me, O Love,
As I have bowed to Thee,
Through countless ages.

The veil of separation is torn,
O Beloved, Thou and I are One.

XII

As the aspen leaf is aquiver
With the breeze,
So my heart dances with Thy love.
As two mountain streams meet
With a roar,
Joyous in their exultation,
So have I met Thee, O my Beloved.

As the mountain top is aglow
At the going down of the sun,
Giving to the valley an immense desire,
So hast Thou given glory to my being.
As the valley is still at eventide,
So hast Thou calmed my soul.

My heart is filled
With the love of a thousand years.
Mine eyes
Behold Thy vision.

As the stars make the night beauteous,
So hast Thou given beauty to my soul.
As serene as the graven image
Have I become.

As the seed grows into a wondrous tree,
The abode of many joyous birds,
Giving soft shadows
To the weary traveler,
So has my soul grown
In search of Thee.

As a great river joins the sea,
So to Thee have I come,
Rich from my long journey,
Full with the experience of an age.
O Beloved,

As the dewdrop
Mingles with the honey
Of the flower,
So Thou and I have become one.
O my Beloved,
Now there is no separation,
No loneliness,
No sorrow, no struggle.
Where'er I go
I bring the glory of Thy presence.
For, O Beloved,
Thou and I are one.

XIII

As the small stream
Gathers strength on its long journey,
Feeding the lonely plains, the tall drooping trees,
Dancing its way to the open seas,
Attaining liberation—
So have I entered into Thee.

Long has been the journey
On this trackless path of time,
Where every little snag
Gives forth music and the sound of waters,
Where every little pool
Reflects the glory of heavens, to stagnate,
Where every little peaceful spot
Is burdened with the scent of decay.

Long did I struggle
To swim in the strong current;
Many a time, exhausted,
Have I been flung
On the craggy banks of Time.

Weary of all experience,
Gathering strength from that very weariness,

Have I run faster
To where the open waters meet
With a roar,
The small mysterious streams.

Liberated from Time,
Without the limitation of Space,
Have I become as the dewdrop
That creates the vast seas.

Oh! the lotus is unfolding its glory to the morning sun,
I open my heart to Thee, O my Beloved.

XIV

Since I have met with Thee,
O my Beloved,
Never have I known loneliness.

A stranger am I
Amidst all peoples,
In all lands.
Amidst the multitude of strangers,
Full am I
As of the scent of jasmine.
They surround me,
But I know no loneliness.

I weep for the strangers;
How alone they are.
Full of immense loneliness,
Fearful,
They take to themselves
People
As lonely as themselves.

A guest am I
In this world of transient things,
Unfettered by the entanglements thereof.

I am of no country,
No boundaries hold me.

O friend,
I weep for thee.
Thou layest thy foundation,
But thy house perisheth on the morrow.

O friend,
Come with me,
Abide in the house of my Beloved.
Though thou shalt wander the earth,
Possessing nothing,
Thou shalt be as welcome
As the lovely spring,
For thou bringest with thee
The Companion of all.

O friend,
Live with me,
My Beloved and I are one.

XV

It has been given to me,
O friend,
To see the face of my Beloved.

His smile
Has filled my heart.
As the rivers of water
Make constant music,
O friend,
So my being rejoices
In the splendor of His love.

As one beholds the mountain-top
At the setting of the sun,
Radiant and serene

Above the darkening world,
O friend,
So the vision of my Beloved
Has made me
Pure and at peace.

As at the lifting of the dark cloud
From the happy face of the mountain,
O friend,
So the shadow of life
Has lifted
At the approach of my well-Beloved.

As the mists of the morn
Are consumed by the warm rays,
O friend,
So my well-Beloved
Has gathered me in,
Dispelling the vision of emptiness.

As the deep valley lies
In the shadow of a great mountain,
O friend,
So I lie
In the shadow of the hand
Of my well-Beloved.

As the rose
Amidst many thorns,
O friend, so am I
Amidst passing things.

As the day is made glorious
By the darkness of the night,
By the light of the day,
O friend,
So have I been made glorious.

As the rivers are full
After the great rains,

O friend,
So has my well-Beloved
Burdened me with His love.

The ages have awaited this hour.
I have met with my Beloved.

XVI

O my Beloved,
Thou art Liberation,
The end of all desire,
The consummation of love.

O my Beloved,
Thou art the unfading beauty of Truth,
Thou art the accomplishment of all thought,
Thou art the flower of all devotion.

O my Beloved,
O my Love,
The sun is beyond the purple hills,
And as a single star
I have risen
In Thine adoration.

Thou and I,
We have well met.
O my Beloved,
Art Thou not myself?
Art Thou not the perfume of my heart?

I am Thy Beloved,
My Beloved art Thou.
Thou art my companion of ages.
I am Thy shadow,
In the garden of eternity.

XVII

As divinity lies hidden in a flower,
So my Beloved dwells in me.
As thunder is among the mountains,
So is my Beloved within my heart.
As the cry of a bird in a still forest,
So has the voice of my Beloved filled me.

As fair as the morning,
As serene as the moon,
As clear as the sun,
Is my love for my Beloved.

As the sun goes down
Beyond the purple hills,
Amidst great clouds
And the whispering breeze among the trees,
So has my Beloved descended into me,
To the rejoicing of my heart,
To the glory of my mind.

As of a dark night
Man guides himself
By the distant stars,
So my Beloved guides me
On the waters of life.

Yea, I have sought my Beloved,
And discovered Him seated in my heart.
My Beloved beholds through mine eyes,
For now my Beloved and I are one.

I laugh with Him,
With Him I play.

This shadow is not of mine,
It belongs to the heart of my Beloved,
For now my Beloved and I are One.

THE SONG OF LIFE

The attainment of Truth is an absolute, final experience. I have re-created myself after Truth. I am not a poet; I have merely attempted to put into words the manner of my realization.

I

Make of thy desire the desire of the world,
Of thy love the love of the world.
In thy thoughts take the world to thy mind,
In thy doings let the world behold thine eternity.

Thou mayest draw the many waters of a well,
But thou canst not quench the thirst of thy desires.
Thy heart may hold the flower of its love,
But with the coming of death the flower fadeth.
Thy thoughts may soar to lofty purpose,
But with anxious conflict they are caught in bondage.

As an arrow shot by a strong arm,
So let thy purpose strike deep into the everlasting.
As the mountain stream, pure in its swiftness,
So let thy mind race eagerly towards freedom.

Awakened from the heart of love,
My voice is the voice of understanding,
Born of infinite sorrow.

II

Who can say if thy heart be clean?
Who can tell thee if thy mind be pure?
Who can give thee the satisfaction of thy desire?
Who can heal thee of the burning pain of satisfaction?
Shall understanding be given
Or the way of love be shown to thee?
Shalt thou escape that fear which men call death?
Canst thou put away the ache of loneliness
Or run from the cry of anxiety?
Canst thou hide thyself behind the laughter of music?
Or lose thyself in merry rejoicings?

Wisdom shall be born of understanding.
She putteth forth her voice
In the wilderness of utter confusion.

A man saw the dancing shadows
And went in search of the cause of so much beauty.

Can Life die?
Look into the eye of thy neighbor.

The valley lies hidden in the darkness of a cloud,
But the mountain top is serene
In its gaze of the open sky.

On the banks of a holy river
A pilgrim repeats a ceaseless chant,
And cloistered in a cool temple
A man kneels, lost in a devout whisper.
But, behold, under the heavy dust of summer
Lies a green leaf.

Who shall call thee out of thy prison house?
Or tear away the bondage from thine eyes?
A path mounts slowly up the mountain side,
But who shall carry thee as his burden?

I saw a lame man coming towards me,
I shed tears of aching memory.

In the far distance
A lone star holds the sky.

III

The end is in the beginning of all things,
Suppressed and hidden,
Awaiting to be released through the rhythm
Of pain and pleasure.

Caught in the agony of Time,
Maimed by the inward stress of growth,
O Beloved,
The Self of which thou art the whole
Is seeking the way of illumined ecstasy.

Fashioned in the poetry of balance,
Gathering the riches of life's pursuit,
O Beloved,
The Self of which thou art the whole
Is making its way to the heart of all things.

In the secret sanctuary of desire,
Through the recesses of enfolding love,
O Beloved,
The Self of which thou art the whole
Dances to the Song of Eternity.

By the visible and invisible infinity,
In the round of birth and death,
O Beloved,
The Self of which thou art the whole
Is bridging the space of separation.

Confused in fervent worship,
Deluded by the vain pursuits of thought,
O Beloved,

The Self of which thou art the whole
Is being fused into the Incorruptible.

As ever, O Beloved,
The Self is still the whole.

IV

Listen, O friend,
I shall tell thee of the secret perfume of Life.

Life has no philosophy,
No cunning systems of thought.

Life has no religion,
No adoration in deep sanctuaries.

Life has no god,
Nor the burden of fearsome mystery.

Life has no abode,
Nor the aching sorrow of ultimate decay.

Life has no pleasure, no pain,
Nor the corruption of pursuing love.

Life is neither good nor evil,
Nor the dark punishment of careless sin.

Life gives no comfort,
Nor does it rest in the shrine of oblivion.

Life is neither spirit nor matter,
Nor is there the cruel division of action and inaction.

Life has no death,
Nor has it the void of loneliness in the shadow of Time.

Free is the man who lives in the Eternal,
For Life is.

V

A thousand eyes with a thousand views,
A thousand hearts with a thousand loves,
Am I.

As the sea that receiveth
The clean and the impure rivers
And heedeth not,
So am I.

Deep is the mountain lake,
Clear are the waters of the spring,
And my love is the hidden source of things.

Ah, come hither and taste of my love;
Then, as of a cool evening
The lotus is born,
Shalt thou find thy heart's own secret desire.

The scent of the jasmine fills the night air;
Out of the deep forest
Comes the call of a passing day.

The Life of my love is unburdened;
The attainment thereof is the freedom of fulfillment.

VI

Love is its own divinity.
If thou shalt follow it,
Putting aside the weary burden
Of a cunning mind,
Thou shalt be free of the fear
Of anxious love.

Love is not hedged about
By space and time,
By joyless things of the mind.

Such love delights in the heart
Of him who has richly wandered
In the confusion of love's own pursuits.

The Self, the Beloved,
The hidden loveliness of all things,
Is love's immortality.

O, why needst thou seek further,
Why further, friend?
In the dust of careless love
Lies Life's endless journey.

VII

Love Life.
Neither the beginning nor the end
Knows whence it comes.
For it has no beginning and no end.
Life is.

In the fulfilling of Life there is no death,
Nor the ache of great loneliness.
The voice of melody, the voice of desolation,
Laughter and the cry of sorrow,
Are but Life on its way to fulfillment.

Look into the eyes of thy neighbor
And find thyself with Life;
Therein is immortality,
Life eternal, never changing.

For him who is not in love with Life,
There is the anxious burden of doubt
And the lone fear of solitude;
For him there is but death.

Love Life, and thy love shall know of no corruption.
Love Life, and thy judgment shall uphold thee.
Love Life; thou shalt not wander away
From the path of understanding.

As the fields of the earth are divided,
Man makes a division of Life
And thereby creates sorrow.

Worship not the ancient gods
With incense and flowers,
But Life with great rejoicing;
Shout in the ecstasy of joy
There is no entanglement in the dance of Life.

I am of that Life, immortal, free;
The Eternal Source.
Of that Life I sing.

VIII

Seek not the perfume of a single heart
Nor dwell in its easeful comfort;
For therein abides
The fear of loneliness.

I wept,
For I saw
The loneliness of a single love.

In the dancing shadows
Lay a withered flower.

The worship of many in the one
Leads to sorrow.
But the love of the one in many
Is everlasting bliss.

IX

How easily
The tranquil pool is disturbed
By the passing winds.

Nay, friend,
Seek not thy happiness
In the fleeting.

There is but one way;
That path lies in thyself,
Through thine own heart.

X

A dream comes through a multitude of desires.
When the mind is tranquil,
Undisturbed by thought,
When the heart is chaste
With the fullness of love uncorrupted,
Then shalt thou discover,
O friend,
A world beyond the illusion of words.

Therein is unity of all Life.
Therein is the silent Source
Which sustains the dancing worlds.

In that world there is neither heaven nor hell,
Past, present nor future;
Neither the deception of thought,
Nor the soft whisperings of dying love.

O, seek that world
Where death does not dance in its shadowless ecstasy,
Where the manifestations of Life
Are as the shadows that the smooth lake holds.

It lies about thee
And without thee it exists not.

XI

As out of the deep womb of a mountain
Is born a swift-running stream;
So out of the aching depths of my heart
Has come forth joyous love,
The perfume of the world.

Through the sunlit valleys rush the waters,
Entering lake upon lake,
Ever wandering, never still;
So is my love,
Emptying itself from heart to heart.

As the waters move sadly
Through the dark, cavernous valley;
So has my love become dull
Through the shame of easy desire.

As the tall trees are destroyed
By the strong rush of waters
That have nourished their deep roots,
So has my love torn cruelly
The heart of its rejoicing.

I have shattered the very rock on which I grew.
And as a wide river
Now escapes to the dancing sea, whose waters know no bondage;
So is my love in the perfection of its freedom.

XII

O, rejoice!
There is thunder among the mountains,
And long shadows lie across the green face of the valley.

The rains
Bring forth green shoots
Out of the dead stumps of yesterday.

High among the rocks
An eagle is building his nest.

All things are great with Life.

O friend,
Life fills the world.
Thou and I are in eternal union.

Life is as the waters
That satisfy the thirst of kings and beggars alike:
The golden vessel for the king,
For the beggar the potter's vessel
Which breaks to pieces at the fountain.
Each holds his vessel dear.

There is loneliness,
There is fear of solitude,
The ache of a dying day,
The sorrow of a passing cloud.

Life, destitute of love,
Wanders from house to house,
With none to declare its loveliness.

Out of the granite rock
Is fashioned a graven image
Which men hold sacred;
But they tread carelessly the rock
On the way
That leads to the temple.

O friend,
Life fills the world.
Thou and I are in eternal union.

XIII

Search out the secret pursuit of thy desire;
Then thou shalt not live in illusion.

What canst thou know of happiness,
If in the vale of misery thou hast not walked?

What canst thou know of freedom,
If against thy bondage thou hast not cried aloud?
What canst thou know of love,
If from the entanglement of love
Thou hast not sought deliverance?

I saw the flowers blossom
In the dark hours of a still night.

XIV

Does the raindrop hold in its fullness
The raging stream?
Does the raindrop in its loneliness
Feed the solitary tree on the hill?
Does the raindrop in its great descent
Create the sweet sound of many waters?
Does the raindrop in its pureness
Quench the aching thirst?

It is the unwise who chase
The shadow of self in Life.
And Life eludes them,
For they wander in the ways of bondage.

Wherefore the struggle in loneliness of division?
In Life there is neither you nor I.

XV

I have no name;
I am as the fresh breeze of the mountains.
I have no shelter;
I am as the wandering waters.
I have no sanctuary, like the dark gods;
Nor am I in the shadow of deep temples.
I have no sacred books,
Nor am I well-seasoned in tradition.

I am not in the incense
Mounting on high altars,
Nor in the pomp of ceremonies.
I am neither in the graven image
Nor in the rich chant of a melodious voice.

I am not bound by theories,
Nor corrupted by beliefs.
I am not held in the bondage of religions,
Nor in the pious agony of their priests.
I am not entrapped by philosophies,
Nor held in the power of their sects.

I am neither low nor high,
I am the worshipper and the worshipped.
I am free.

My song is the song of the river
Calling for the open seas,
Wandering, wandering.

I am Life.

XVI

Love not the shapely branch,
Nor place its image alone in thy heart.
It dieth away.

Love the whole tree.
Then thou shalt love the shapely branch,
The tender and the withered leaf,
The shy bud and the full-blown flower,
The falling petal and the dancing height,
The splendid shadow of full love.

Ah, love Life in its fullness.
It knoweth no decay.

XVII

Sorrow is soon forgotten
And pleasure is bound by tears.
None but the clear-eyed shall remember
The deep wounds of their passing sighs.

Sorrow is the shadow
In the wake of pleasure.
Desire is young in its anxious flight;
The swiftness of its deeds
Shall uncover the source of joy.

The conflict of discontent is suffering;
The inviting of sorrow
Is the way to happiness.

Life's dwelling place
Is in the heart of man.

XVIII

Ah, the symphony of that song!
The innermost shrine
Is breathless with the love of many.
The flame dances with the thoughts of many.

The scent of burnt camphor fills the air;
The careless priest drones a chant;
The idol sparkles, seeming to move,
Weary of such boundless adoration.

A still silence holds the air.
And on the instant
A melodious song of infinite heart
Brings untold tears to my eyes.

In a white robe
A woman sings to the heart of her love

Of the travail she knew not,
Of the laughter of children around her breast,
Of the love that died young,
Of the sorrow in a barren home,
Of the solitude in a still night,
Of life fruitless amidst the flowering earth.

I cry with her.
Her heart became mine.

She leaves that abode of sanctity,
Eager with the joy of worship on the morrow.

I follow her through the eternity of time.

O love,
Thou and I shall wander
On the open road of true love.
Thou and I shall never part.

XIX

I have lived the good and evil of men,
And dark became the horizon of my love.

I have known the morality and immorality of men,
And cruel became my anxious thought.

I have shared in the piety and impiety of men,
And heavy became the burden of life.

I have pursued the race of the ambitious,
And vain became the glory of life.

And now I have fathomed the secret purpose of desire.

XX

Out of the fullness of thy heart
Invite sorrow,
And the joy thereof shall be in abundance.

As the streams swell
After the great rains,
And the pebbles rejoice once again
In the murmur of running waters,
So shall thy wanderings by the wayside
Fill the emptiness that createth fear.
Sorrow shall unfold the weaving of life;
Sorrow shall give the strength of loneliness;
Sorrow shall open unto thee
The closed doors of thy heart.

The cry of sorrow is the voice of fulfillment,
And the rejoicing therein
Is the fullness of Life.

XXI

I look to none beside Thee,
O my Beloved.
Thou art born in me,
And lo, there
I take my refuge.

I have read of Thee in many books.
They tell me
That there are many like unto Thee,
That many temples are built for Thee,
That there are many rites
To invoke Thee.
But I have no communion with them,
For all these are but the shells
Of man's thoughts.

O friend,
Seek for the Well-beloved
In the secret recesses of thy heart.
Dead is the tabernacle
When the heart ceases to dance.

I look to none beside Thee,
O my Beloved.
Thou art born in me,
And lo, there
I take my refuge.

XXII

My brother died;
We were as two stars in a naked sky.

He was like me,
Burnt by the warm sun
In the land where are soft breezes,
Swaying palms,
And cool rivers,
Where there are shadows numberless,
Bright-colored parrots and chattering birds.

Where green tree-tops
Dance in the brilliant sun;
Where there are golden sands
And blue-green seas:

Where the world lives in the burden of the sun,
And the earth is baked dull brown;
Where the green-sparkling rice fields
Are luscious in slimy waters,
And shining, brown, naked bodies
Are free in the dazzling light:

The land
Of the mother suckling her babe by the roadside;
Of the devout lover
Offering gay flowers;
Of the wayside shrine;
Of intense silence;
Of immense peace.

He died;
I wept in loneliness.
Where'er I went, I heard his voice
And his happy laughter.
I looked for his face
In every passer-by
And asked each if he had met with my brother;
But none could give me comfort.

I worshipped,
I prayed,
But the gods were silent.
I could weep no more;
I could dream no more.
I sought him in all things,
In every clime.

I heard the whispering of many trees
Calling me to his abode.

And then,
In my search,
I beheld Thee,
O Lord of my heart;
In Thee alone
I saw the face of my brother.

In Thee alone,
O my eternal Love,
Do I behold the faces
Of all the living and all the dead.

XXIII

I tell thee,
Orthodoxy is set up
When the mind and heart are in decay.

As the quiet pool of the woods
Lies hidden under a green mantle,

So is Life covered by the accumulation
Of autumnal thought.

As the soft leaf is heavy with the dust
Of last summer,
So is Life weary
With a dying love.

When thought and feeling are hedged about
By the fear of corruption,
Then, O friend,
Thou art caught in the darkness
Of a fading day.

A tender leaf lies withering
In the shadow of a great valley.

XXIV

As a flower holds the scent,
So do I contain thee,
O World,
In my heart.

Keep me within thy heart,
For I am Liberation,
The unending happiness of Life.

As a precious stone
Lies deep in the earth,
So am I hidden
Deep in thy heart.

Though thou dost not know me,
I know thee full well.
Though thou dost not think of me,
My world is filled with thee.
Though thou dost not love me,
Thou art my unchanging love.
Though thou worshippest me

In temples, churches and mosques,
I am a stranger to thee;
But thou art my eternal companion.
As the mountains protect
The peaceful valley,
So do I cover thee,
O World,
With the shadow of my hand.

As the rains come
To a parched land,
So, O World,
Do I come
With the scent of my love.

Keep thy heart
Pure and simple,
O world,
For then thou shalt welcome me.

I am thy love,
The desire of thy heart.

Keep thy mind
Tranquil and clear,
O World,
For therein is thine own understanding.

I am thine understanding,
The fullness
Of thine own experience.

I sit in the temple,
I sit by the wayside,
Watching the shadows move
From place to place.

XXV

Reason is the treasure of the mind,
Love is the perfume of the heart;

Yet both are of one substance,
Though cast in different molds.

As a golden coin
Bears two images
Parted by a thin wall of metal,
So between love and reason
Is the poise of understanding,
That understanding
Which is of both mind and heart.

O life, O Beloved,
In Thee alone is eternal love,
In Thee alone is everlasting thought.

XXVI

As the spark
That shall give warmth
Is hid among the gray ashes,
So, O friend,
The light
Which shall guide thee
Under the dust
Of thine experience.

XXVII

O friend,
Thou canst not bind Truth.

It is as the air,
Free, limitless,
Indestructible,
Immeasurable.

It hath no dwelling place,
Neither temple nor altar.

It is of no one God,
However zealous be His worshippers.

Canst thou tell
From what single flower
The bee gathereth the sweet honey?

O friend,
Leave heresy to the heretic,
Religion to the orthodox;
But gather Truth
From the dust of thine experience.

XXVIII

As the potter
To the joy of his heart
Molds the clay;
So canst thou create
To the glory of thy being
Thy future.

As the man of the forest
Cuts a path
Through the thick jungle;
So canst thou make,
Through this turmoil of affliction,
A clear path
To thy freedom from sorrows,
To thy lasting happiness.

O friend,
As for a moment
The mysterious mountains
Are concealed by the passing mists;
So art thou hid
In the darkness
Of thy creation.
The fruit of the seed thou sowest
Shall burden thee.

O friend,
Heaven and hell
Are words
To frighten thee to right action;
But heaven and hell exist not.
Only the seeds of thine own actions
Shall bring into being
The flower of thy longing.

As the maker of images
Carves the human shape
Out of granite,
So, out of the rock
Of thine experience,
Hew thine eternal happiness.

Thy life is a death;
Death is a rebirth.
Happy is the man
Who is beyond the clutches
Of their limitations.

XXIX

The mountain comes down to the dancing waters,
But its head is hidden in a dark cloud.

On the stump of a dead pine
There grew a delicate flower.

The substance of my love is Life
And in its pathway there is no death.

XXX

Doubt is as a precious ointment;
Though it burns, it shall heal greatly.

I tell thee, invite doubt
When in the fullness of thy desire.

Call to doubt
At the time when thine ambition
Is outrunning others in thought.
Awaken doubt
When thy heart is rejoicing in great love.

I tell thee,
Doubt brings forth eternal love;
Doubt cleanses the mind of its corruption.
So the strength of thy days
Shall be established in understanding.

For the fullness of thy heart,
And for the flight of thy mind,
Let doubt tear away thine entanglements.

As the fresh winds from the mountains
That awaken the shadows in the valley,
So let doubt call to dance
The decaying love of a contented mind.

Let not doubt enter darkly thy heart.

I tell thee,
Doubt is as a precious ointment;
Though it burns, it shall heal greatly.

XXXI

Listen to me,
O friend.

Be thou a yogi, a monk, a priest,
A devout lover of God,
A pilgrim searching for happiness,
Bathing in holy rivers,
Visiting sacred shrines,
The occasional worshipper of a day,
A reader of many books,
Or a builder of temples,

My love aches for thee.
I know the way to the heart of the Beloved.

This vain struggle,
This long toil,
This ceaseless sorrow,
This changing pleasure,
This burning doubt,
This burden of life:
All these will cease, O friend.
My love aches for thee.
I know the way to the heart of the Beloved.

Have I wandered over the earth,
Have I loved the reflections,
Have I chanted, rapt in ecstasy,
Have I donned the robe,
Have I listened to the temple bells,
Have I grown heavy with study,
Have I searched,
Have I been lost?
Yea, much have I known.
My love aches for thee.
I know the way to the heart of the Beloved.

O friend,
Wouldst thou love the many reflections,
If thou canst have reality?
Throw away thy bells, thine incense,
Thy fears and thy gods;
Set aside thy creeds, thy philosophies;

Come,
Put aside all these:
I know the way to the heart of the Beloved.

O friend,
The simple union is the best.
That is the way to the heart of the Beloved.

XXXII

Through the veil of Form,
O Beloved,
I see Thee, myself in manifestation.

How unattainable are the mountains to the valley,
Though the mountains hold the valley!
How mysterious is the darkness
That brings forth the watching stars,
And yet the night is born of day!

I am in love with Life.
As the mountain lake
Which receives many streams
And sends forth great rivers,
But holds its unknown depths,
So is my love.

Calm and clear, as the mountains in the morning
Is my thought,
Born of love.

Happy is the man who has found the harmony of Life,
For then he creates in the light of eternity.

PARABLES

I

TOYS

A child
Had arranged on the polished floor
Its toys, neatly and with care.
The drum,
The bugles,
The cannons,
The soldiers,
And an officer with much gold—
Undoubtedly a field-marshal—
The long train
With its polished engine,
A tiny airplane,
A big automobile,
These were on one side.

On the other,
A doll with curly hair,
Dressed in the latest fashion,
Its bare knees showing,
Black polished shoes
With silk stockings.

A little further away,
Men in long coats and top hats.
A bag
With a string
To bind them all.

The child had gone.

Then up sprang a man
In long coat, with his hat in hand:
"I represent God,
And all of you listen.
I have discovered
Heaven and Hell.
All who obey
Go to Heaven and to the Paradise of Gods,
But those who disobey
To Hell and to great sorrows.

I know who is fit and worthy of Heaven,
I alone can give spiritual distinctions and spiritual titles,
I alone can make a man happy or unhappy,
I alone can introduce God to you,
I alone know the path to Him,
I am the priest of God."

"I am the protector, the ruler
And the dispenser of life,
I, with my friends the merchants,
Decide to wage wars, to kill and to slaughter,
To protect you, my friends, from your enemies.
Our country is above all.
Woe to all who do not kill,
Who do not wear uniform,
Who are unpatriotic—which I decide.
God is on our side,
He waves the only flag—our flag—"
Roared the man with the sword and many ribbons.

Then a large fat man spoke quietly:
"You two may say what you please,

I hold the monies.
I am the dispenser of all things,
Of temporal power,
Of cruelty and kindness,
Of progress and evolution,
Without me nothing shall be decided.
I am a man of great wealth,
Thy wealth shalt be the only God,
I have finished."

Then the man whom nobody noticed,
Spoke:
"I can destroy all your Gods,
Your theories and your wealth,
Without me you can do nothing.
You cannot talk to me of God
When I am hungry,
Feed me and I will listen to your Gods.
You cannot make me
Into cannon fodder.
Pay me and excite me
And I shall fight.
You are rich because of me,
I toil for you, suffer for you,
Go hungry for you and die for you,
I am your food and your comfort,
Your love and your destroyer,
I am going to strip you of all these,
Now I strike."

Then the lady with bare knees—
"I am laughing
Because each of you thinks
You are the most important.
Glorying in your own importance
Where would you all be without me?
Still in that Heaven or Hell
Of which you spoke, O friend with the long coat.
I am your sister, your mother,

Your wife and your love.
I am on the stage of your bestial amusement,
I bear children—the agony of it—for your pleasure,
I dress showing just enough
For your pleasure,
I paint and make a fool of myself
For your pleasure,
I covet your glances and long for your love,
I desire children without you,
I seek freedom in spite of you,
I struggle to be free of your desires,
To show my equality,
I do things that astonish you,
I shall usurp all your places,
Your honors, your glories.
You worship me,
You desecrate me.
I am a woman
But your master."

Then all began to talk,
Advancing this complicated theory and that complicated theory,
This solution and that solution,
Class against class,
Wealth against poverty,
Hungry against the well-fed.

A roar and utter chaos.

The child came back,
Gathered up its toys,
Knocking down one or two
In its hurry.
Then it went out,
Laughing.

II

There is a mountain, far beyond the plains and hills, whose great
   summit overlooks the dark valley and the open seas.
Neither cloud nor deep mists ever hide its calm face. It is above the
   shadows of day and night.
From the vast plain, no man can behold it. Some have seen it but
   there be few that have reached its feet.
One in many thousand years gathers his strength and gains that
   abode of eternity.
I speak of that mountain top, serene, infinite, beyond thought.
I shout for joy!

One day, a man beheld through the opening of a cloud, the calm face
of the mountain. He stopped every passer-by, that would stay to give
an answer, and inquired of the way that would lead him beyond the
mists. Some said take this path, and others said take that path. After
many days of confusion and toil, he arrived among the hills.

A man, full in years, wise in the ways of the hills, said, "I know the
way. You cannot reach the mountain, O friend, unless you are strength-
ened by the power that comes from the adoration of the image in yonder
shrine."

Many days passed in peaceful worship.

Tired of worship, he asked of men that seemed great with under-
standing.

"Yea," said one, "I know the way. But if you would gain the fulfill-
ment of your desire, carry this on you. It will uphold you in your
weariness." He gave him the symbol of his struggle.

Another cried, "Yea, I know the way. But many days of contempla-
tion must be passed in the seclusion of a sanctuary, with my picture of
eternity."

"I know the way," said another, "But you must perform these rites,
understand these hidden laws, you must enter the association of the
elect and hold fast to the knowledge that we shall give you."

"Be loud in the song of praise of the reflection that you seek," said
another.

"Come, follow me, obeying all things I say. I know the way," cried
another.

In the long last, the calm face of the mountain was utterly forgotten. Now he wanders from hill to hill, crying aloud, "Yes, I know the way, but. . . ."

There is a mountain far beyond the plains and hills whose summit overlooks the dark valley and the open seas. Neither cloud nor deep mists ever hide its calm face. It is above the shadows of day and night.
One in many thousand years gathers his strength and gains that abode of eternity.
I speak of that mountain top, serene, infinite, beyond thought.
I shout for joy!

III

In my garden there is life and death, the laughter of many flowers and the cry of falling petals.
A dead tree and a green tree look on each other.
It is mid-summer and the shadows are dancing save about the dead tree.
The song of waters shall not set it a-dancing, nor the rain bring forth the hidden leaves.
Ah, it is so bare, so empty!
Who shall nourish it, who shall caress it with life?
The far skies look down on the dead and the living.
Through the long suffering winter, lies concealed a seed of lovely promise. Cold winds, tearing gales, noisy storms, hold back the loveliness of the seed. Dark days and sunless hours deny the glory of the seed.
With the soft breeze from the warm south the hidden seed awakens to life.
The song of the birds over the blue skies calls the still seed to life.
The scent of warm rain awakens deep memories of the seed to life.
Through the burden of heavy earth, life breaks forth and rejoices.
It grew by the dusty road-side among the lazy stones.
With its single flower, it danced the day long.
A boy, on his homeward way, uproots it and throws it away.
Creation lies in the path of careless love.

IV

I would like to tell a story.

Once upon a time there was a man who desired to understand the beauty of the moon and the softness of its rays and the causes of these things. So he went forth and gazed into the skies. Between him and the moon there was a lovely tree with a delicate branch and tender leaves. Forgetting the moon, he began to examine the delicate branch and the tender leaves and was lost in the thought of such delicacy, and when he looked up again, the moon had set. The understanding of life is more essential than the mere superficial knowledge of the machinery of life, though one must be acquainted with this also.

V

Once upon a time, when there was great understanding and in the world full rejoicing, there lived a gentle woman, full of years.

One day, she found herself in a temple, before the altar made by the human hand. She was crying bitterly to heaven and none was there to comfort her. Till in the long last, a friend of God took notice of her and asked the reason for her tears.

"God must have forgotten me. My husband is gracious and well. My children are full and strong. Many servants are there to care for us. All things are well with me and mine own. God has forgotten us."

The friend of God replied, "God never forgets His children."

When she came home, she found her son dead.

She never cried.

"God remembers me and mine own."

VI

The mountains look on the town and the town looks upon the sea.

It was the time of many flowers and calm blue skies.

In a big house, where the trees gathered around there lived a man, rich in the possession of things. He had visited the capitals of many lands in search of a cure.

He was lame, scarcely able to walk.

A stranger from the distant and sunny lands, came by chance to the town that looks upon the sea.

The lame man and the distant stranger passed by, touching each other in a narrow lane.

The lame man was healed, and the town whispered in amazement.

On the next day, the man made whole was taken to prison for some immorality.

VII

There is a little town, sheltered in the shadow of a great mountain.

There are many people in that town and only one street with numerous shops.

The shop of gay and bright colored flowers, to which people came with laughter in their hearts—

The shop where they sell clothes, a delight to the vanity of the people who come out of it—

The shop where they sell toys; grave men and little children enter in.

Outside the large shop where food is sold, a beggar waits.

There is a gloomy house which undertakes to rid the people of their dead. How prosperous are they that live within!—

A house where they sell God; where they teach the people fear, and then the way to overcome their fear. In that house there are many dark corridors in which worshippers lose themselves. A man, in gorgeous robes, tells of the beauty of an unknown Deity.

There is a well-built house where they keep in perfect order the dead creations of the past.

One day, when there were many joyous shadows, a stranger came and the people were delighted with his visit, for there came few strangers to that town.

They feasted him in honor and the town rejoiced.

They showed him their shops, their house of gloom and the gilded building where God was kept for sale.

In the street there is a procession of mourners for the dead.

The people looked to the stranger for a passing word of comfort, but behold, he laughs.

For he is in love with Life and death passes him by.

They understood him not but hurried him out of their gates.

The stranger climbs to the mountain top, which overlooks that crowded town.

VIII

There was, once on a time, a man whose heart rejoiced in Life. He loved Life and therefore he loved all things.

He was a friend to the meanest and to the greatest.

For is not Life as the waters which satisfy the thirst of the wise and the foolish?

Now this man was greatly sought after for his understanding in wisdom.

One day, when the skies were blue and the sun was warm, the ants came out of their deep nests and wandered on the face of the land, so that the pathway was moving with them.

In his far-seeing wisdom the lover of Life saw a man drowning in the smiling, blue lake. He hastened on the pathway, to save him from the dancing waters, thereby crushing many ants.

The people were troubled, for said they, "How can this man be a true lover of Life when he destroys? How foolish we are to look to him for love."

He wanders lonely among the mountains.

Ah, how little they love!

IX

THE MASTER SINGER OF LIFE

On the banks of a soft running river
There was a village full of people but empty of life.
Oh, the sorrow of it!

Many were the tall temples with graven images,
Gods molded after the thought of man,

Proud priests, soft of voice, loud in chants,
Grave talkers of philosophy, under the cool trees;
The cry of burden, the fear of sorrow,
Complicated laws of religion,
Morality made for others,
The strong maintained by the weak.
The naked and the clothed walked on the same narrow street,
All in strife one against another,
Their Gods, their laws and their love.

They called the village the world.

On a fair day, at the meeting of four roads,
A man cried,
"Listen, O people,
There is a corruption, and a strife;
The song of your life is impure.
The Master Singer of Life
Comes to this ancient village;
Harken to the harmony of his song."

The jasmine opens its heart to the dark night.

"I am the Master Singer of Life,
I have suffered long, I know.
Keep pure the song in thy heart,
Simple is the way.
Be rid of the complexities of Gods, of religions and of beliefs
    therein.
Bind not thy life with rites, with the desire after comfort.
Be a lamp unto thyself. Thou shalt not then cast a shadow across
    the face of another.
Life cannot be held in the bondage of fear.
Be free, then there shall be the miracle of order.
Love life, then there shall be no loneliness.
Ah, listen to the voice of my love;
I have suffered long, I know.
I am free, eternally happy;
I am the Master Singer of Life."

Softly falls the rain on the burning land.

A few listened and greatly rejoiced.
Putting aside all things
They freed life of all bondage.

"Yea," cried the people,
"But how shall we reconcile the beauty of our Gods with thy song?
In what manner shall we fit thy sayings into the temples of our
  creation?
Thou art the bringer of confusion.
We shall have none of thee,
Thou sayest things that we know not,
What thou sayest is of the Devil,
Away, away."

The Master Singer of Life went on his way,
And the people struggled with the problem of reconciliation.

X

A FABLE

Once upon a time—which is the way in which all true stories begin
—there was a world in which all the people were sick and sad, and yet
all of them were seeking to be released from their suffering and to find
happiness. In search of this happiness they prayed, they worshipped,
they loved and they hated, they married and made wars. They begot
children as miserable as themselves and yet they taught those children
that happiness was their right and their eventual goal.

Then one day in the midst of this suffering world there rose a
whisper, which grew into a shout, that a Great Teacher was coming
who, because of his love for the world and because of his wisdom,
would bring to those who were suffering, comfort in their sorrow, and
would show all the people in the world how they might find the lasting
happiness which all were seeking.

And in order to spread widely the glad news of the coming of the
Teacher, organizations and societies were formed, and men and women
went throughout the world telling of the Teacher who would come.
Some prayed to him that he would come more quickly. Some performed
ceremonies in order to prepare the world to receive him. Some made
profound studies of forgotten times, when other great Teachers had

come and taught, so that by this study they might better understand him. Some proclaimed themselves his disciples in advance, so that when he came there might be some at least to stand around him and to understand him.

Then one day he came. And he told the people of the world that he had come to bring them happiness, to heal their pain and to soothe their sorrows. He said that he himself, through much suffering and pain, had found his way to an abode of peace, to a Kingdom of eternal Joy. He told them that he had come to lead them and to guide them to that abode. But, he said, because the path leading to that Kingdom was steep and narrow, only those could follow him who were willing to set aside everything that they had accumulated in the past. He asked them to set aside their Gods, their religions, their rites and ceremonies, their books and their knowledge, their families and friends. And if they would do that, he said, he would provide them with food for the journey, he would satisfy their burning thirst with the living water he possessed, and would bring them into the Kingdom of Happiness where he himself dwelt eternally.

Then those people, who for so many years had been preparing for the Teacher, began to feel uncomfortable and troubled. For they said: "This is not the teaching we expected and for which we have been preparing. How can we renounce all this knowledge which we have so painfully acquired? Without it the world would never understand the Teacher. How can we renounce all these splendid rites and ceremonies in the performing of which we find so much happiness and power? How can we renounce our families and friends when we need them so much? What teaching is this?"

And they began to question among themselves: "Can this indeed be the Teacher whom we have been expecting? We never thought he would speak in this way and ask of us such renunciations." And those especially who had proclaimed themselves his disciples, because of their more intimate knowledge of his will, felt uncomfortable and troubled.

Then after much thought and meditation light came to them and a solution of their difficulties. And they said: "It is true that the Teacher comes to help the world, but we know the world better than he does and so we will act as his interpreters to the world."

And so those who had knowledge said: "His call for renunciation does not apply to us because the world needs our knowledge and could not do without it, so for the sake of the world we shall go on seeking knowledge."

And those who performed rites and ceremonies said: "We have of course renounced all rites and ceremonies for our own benefit, we have passed beyond any need of them, but for the sake of the world we shall continue to perform them, otherwise the world would suffer." So they continued to build Churches and Temples and to perform rites, all to help the world, and they were too busy to listen to the Teacher.

And the only people who willingly renounced were those who gave up their homes and their families because they wanted freedom from duty and obligation. And they came to the Teacher and said: "We have left all to follow you, now find us an easy job where we can work for you and also earn a living."

Some there were, a few, who set aside all things, and sat at the feet of the Teacher, and tried to learn from him how they might feed the hungry and satisfy the thirsty. These people thought that his wisdom was likely to prove more helpful to the world than their knowledge; that his simplicity might be more easily understood than their complications; that the Teacher might know best when he said that rites and ceremonies were not necessary for the finding of the happiness he came to give; that you could renounce your family and friends in your heart while not deserting them in the flesh.

But the others reproached them for their selfishness and idleness. They said: "The world does not need the bread of the Teacher, but a particular kind of pastry for which we hold the recipe. It does not need water to quench its thirst, but the wine contained in our chalices. The words of your Teacher will not help the world, because they are too simple and the world cannot understand what they mean. We have complicated theories to solve the complicated problems of the world and the world can understand them."

So there were few of those who had most eagerly announced the coming of the Teacher who listened to the teaching he gave. There were some who said: "This is not the Teacher we expected, so we will go on preparing for the coming of the real Teacher." And the others built up walls and barriers round him so that none could get to him unless they opened the gates.

So in a few years he went away and then the same people hailed him as divinely inspired, and they built new Churches in his name and invented new and elaborate rites and ceremonies for his glory, and built a new religion upon the teaching he had not given. And the world continued to suffer and cry for help.

PROSE POEMS

I

A HYMN

I have stood in Thy holy presence,
I have seen the splendor of Thy face,
I prostrate at Thy sacred feet,
I kiss the hem of Thy garment,
I have felt the glory of Thy beauty,
I have seen Thy serene look.

Thy wisdom has opened my closed eyes,
Thine eternal peace has transfigured me.
Thy tenderness, the tenderness of a mother to her child, the teacher
    to his pupil, I have felt.
Thy compassion for all things, living and non-living, the animate
    and inanimate, I have felt.

Thy joy, indescribable, has thrilled me,
Thy voice has opened in me many voices.
Thy touch has awakened my heart.
Thine eyes have opened mine eyes.
Thy glory has kindled the glory in me.
O Master of Masters, I have yearned for this happy hour when I
    should stand in Thy holy presence,
At last it has been granted unto me.

I am happy,
I am peaceful, peaceful as the bottom of a deep blue lake.
I am calm, calm as the snow-clad mountaintop above the storm
    clouds.
I have longed for this hour, it has come.
I shall follow humbly in Thy footsteps along that path which Thy
    holy feet have trodden.
I shall humbly serve the world, the world for which thou hast
    suffered, sacrificed and toiled.
I shall bring that peace into the world.
I have longed for this happy hour, it has come.

Thine image is in mine heart,
Thy compassion is burning in me,
Thy wisdom guides me,
Thy peace enlightens me,
Thy tenderness has given me the power to sacrifice.
Thy love has given me energy.
Thy glory pervades my entire being.

I have yearned for this hour, it has come, in all the splendor of a
    glorious spring.
I am young as the youngest.
I am old as the oldest.
I am happy as a blind lover, for I have found my love.
I have seen.
I can never be blind, though a thousand years pass.
I have seen Thy divine face everywhere, in the stone, in the blade
    of grass, in the giant pines of the forest, in the reptile, in the
    lion, in the criminal, in the saint.
I have longed for this magnificent moment, it came and I have
    grasped it.

I have stood in Thy presence.
I have seen the splendor of Thy face.
I prostrate at Thy sacred feet.
I kiss the hem of Thy garment.

II

The mind well poised,
Calm, serene,
Free from the limitations of prejudice,
My heart dances with Thy love, O Beloved.

How can I forget Thy love?
As well ask the rose
To delight in summer's day
Without its tender petals.

How can I be separated from Thee,
O Guru of Gurus?
As well ask the waters of the sea
To separate from its joyous waves.

If in this world there is loneliness,
Then, where art Thou, O my Love?

As the sun fills the earth
With dancing shadows and great open spots of light,
So hast Thou filled my heart
In great abundance.

III

FIND THY SOUL, O FRIEND

Nay, canst thou tell me,
O friend,
Whence comes this mighty assurance
And the purpose thereof?
The cause of this ceaseless strife,
This violent desire for many possessions,
This immense longing for life,
This never-ending struggle after the passing happiness?

How quickly
Fades the lovely rose.
How easily
O friend,
Sorrow is begotten.

O friend,
Thou wilt find thy lasting happiness
In no temple,
In no book,
Not in the intellect of man,
Nor in the Gods of thy creation.
Go not to holy places,
Worship not in wayside shrines.

How easily
The tranquil pool is disturbed,
And the reflection thereof.

Nay, friend,
Seek not thy happiness
In passing things.
Find thy soul,
O friend,
For there alone
Abideth thy Beloved.

IV

TELL ME, WHICH IS THE REAL?

How suddenly
The still pool is disturbed!
The passing wind
Delights with the restless waters,
The Insect
Makes patterns,
Annoying the tranquil waters.

The reflections
Pass away, to be re-established again,
The stately tree,
The blue heavens,
The swift bird,
The heavy cloud,
The tall house with many windows,
Are there in the quiet pool.

The sun through the green leaves,
The distant stars, through immense space,
My own face, so close,
Are there established.
O pool,
My tears disturb thy waters.
Tell me,
Which is the real?

V

THE BEGGAR AT THE SHRINE

As the beggar,
Lean and hungry,
Sits on the steps of the temple
Shaking his empty bowl,
So have I sat
Crying for my empty heart
To be filled.

The worshippers
On their way to the Shrine,
With the habit of offering,
With a smile,
They gave me of their gifts.

But on the morrow,
With the beggers
I took my place

Once again,
Sad and empty.

VI

COME AWAY

As many scores of rivers
Enter into the sea,
So the understanding of the world
Has come unto me.
An immense longing
Is born unto me,
An aching love
Is burning my heart,
A passionate desire
Is consuming my being.

Come away,
Come away,
O world,
From thy changing sorrows,
From thy dying love.
I have found the way.

Come away,
Come away,
O world,
From thy little Gods,
From thy interpreters thereof.
I have found the way.

Come away,
Come away,
O world,
From thy fleeting passions,
From thy decaying achievements.
I have found the way.

Come away,
Come away,
O world,
From thy prison of pain,
From thy keepers thereof.
I have found the way.

Come away,
Come away,
O world,
From thy burning desires,
From thy agonies therein.
I have found the way.

Come away,
Come away,
O world,
From the false,
From the burdens thereof.
I have found the way.

Come away,
Come away,
O world,
From thy kneeling,
From the holding up of thy sad hands,
The temple walls are falling.
I have found the way.

Come away,
Come away,
O world,
For all things perish,
Though thy soft tears
Wash away thy memories.
I have found the way.

Seized am I
With a burning passion
To free thee

From thy cage,
For I have found the way.

The bird is on the wing,
And his voice fills my heart.
The vast firmament,
The limitless space,
Enfold me.

I am thy lover,
I am thy teacher,
Renounce all
And follow me,
For my way
Is the way of Liberation.

Come,
Come away,
O love,
Sit beside me;
I will teach thee
The way to Happiness.

VII

WALK BY THE LIGHT OF MY LOVE
AND THOU SHALT CAST NO SHADOW

My well-Beloved and I
Hold thee, O friend,
In our heart.
I speak to thee
From the depths of my heart.
I am united with my well-Beloved.
I am as the petal to the rose;
I am as the scent to the jasmine,
My well-Beloved and I
Are inseparable, indivisible.
As the moon reflects the glory of the sun,
So do I reflect the glory of my well-Beloved.

As soft as the shade
Of a moonlit night
So is my love for thee,
O friend.
As the whirlwinds that sweep
O'er the lands,
So is my love
That shall wipe out the darkness about thee.
As the mountain streams
That come down with a roar
Into the valley,
So let my love enter into thee.
As the solitary tree
Amidst the great mountains
Withstands the raging winds,
So shall my love uphold thee
In times of strife and affliction.
As the sea putteth forth mighty waves
And conquereth all things
So shall my love vanquish
The travail of thy life.

Yea, O friend,
Passing exceeding great
Is my love for thee.
Drink of it, thou shalt be no more thirsty.
Eat of it, thou shalt know of no hunger.
Bind it to thy heart, thou shalt not taste of sorrow.
Write it down in the tablet of thy mind,
Thou shalt be the son of wisdom and understanding.
Walk by the light of my love,
Thou shalt cast no shadow.

O friend,
Come unto me,
I will show thee the way of love.
Turn not thy head,
Close not up thine ears,
Seal not up thy heart,

But come after me,
I will lead thee
To the abode of love.
Oh! My heart acheth for thee,
For thou dost not listen
To the voice of my love.
Why dost thou not answer to my call?
Why dost thou walk away from me?
Why dost thou hide thy face among the shadows?
Why dost thou pursue the fleeting
That engendereth in thee sorrow?
Why dost thou hold thyself against me?
Why art thou blind to my love?
Why dost thou eat out of the hand of affliction?
Ah! Answer me,
For I am heavy with love.

The love that begetteth sorrow,
The love that killeth the smile on an open face,
The love that changeth from moment to moment,
The love that's lonely in its solitude,
The love that's haughty and oppressive,
The love that destroyeth the love for others,
The love that binds and places a limitation,
The love that's consumed with the fires of self,
These thou shalt not taste of
If thou walkest with me.

O friend,
What dost thou pursue?
What's the purpose that leadeth thee on?
What shadows entice thee on?
What murmurings urge thee on?
Whither goest thou?

O friend,
The divisions of people,
The oppression of the poor,
The wars of nations,

The exploitation of the ignorant,
The hatred of class against class,
The strife after wealth, and the sorrow thereof,
The intricacy of governments,
The portioning of lands,
All these cease to be
In the clothing of love.

Doth not the man of the fields,
After the labors of the day,
Seek the shelter of love?
Doth not the man of multitudes of things
Grow weary of his possessions
And seek the shelter of love?
Doth not the ruler of many peoples
Suffer the loneliness of his ambitions
And seek the shelter of love?
Doth not the man of the temple,
Caught up in the exhaustion of his worship,
Seek the shelter of love?
Yea,
All are in search of the abode
That giveth them the glory of love.

But why dost thou contest,
O friend,
One against another,
In the pursuit of love?
Why this setting aside of joy
In the hatred of one against another?
Why this consuming envy
That setteth one against another,
And destroyeth utterly thy happiness?

Oh! My heart aches for thee,
O friend.
Keep open wide thy heart,
And let no dark shadows creep therein,
For without love there shall be

Desolation and a strife without an end.
Keep pure thy heart,
For with impurity
There shall be affliction and travail.
I tell thee
That wherever thou art,
Whatever be thy sorrow,
Whatever be thy rejoicing,
The way to the heart of the Beloved
Is the way of love.
For it leadeth thee to simplicity,
And to the faith that conquereth.
Understanding cometh by the way
Of love,
And knowledge therefrom.
Yea,
Love all and therein lose thyself.

My well-Beloved and I
Hold thee, O friend,
In our heart.
I speak to thee
From the depth of my love.
I am as the petal to the rose,
I am as the scent to the jasmine.
I am united with my well-Beloved;
Come unto me:
I am the heart of love.

VIII

MY HEART IS HEAVY WITH THY LOVE

The red, red moon arose
Eastward, o'er the dreaming sea.
The dark palm sighs
With the coming quiet of the night.
The distant cry of a bird

On its homeward flight,
The soft ripple of cool waters
Tapping the warm shores.

A heart burdened
Of frenzied joy, near pain.

A heart of understanding is my need.

A melodious song,
Soft and plaintive,
Cometh up from the deep shadows.
Oppressive grows the quiet night air.

As the far winking light
In the dark temple tower,
Above the worshippers
And their groaning prayers,
High above the silent Gods
Amidst their gloomy abodes,
So have I become,
Free from the hand that wrought me,
The conquerer of aching time
And its sorrowing ways.

O friend,
Come away from the complications of belief,
Destroy the monumental superstitions
Of thy enslaving creed.
But grow in the simplicity of thy heart,
In the shadows of thy suffering.

O Beloved,
My heart is heavy with thy love.

IX

WHO SHALL GIVE THEE COMFORT

Who shall give thee comfort
In the days of thy trouble,

In the days of thy sorrow?
From whom shalt thou seek
The consolation of thy heart,
The satisfaction of thy mind,
In the days of darkness,
In the days of affliction?

As the rain cometh
And falleth on the land
In due season,
So, O friend,
Sorrow descends on all,
And it shall spare none.
The poor who are humble in the ways
Of life,
The wealthy who are arrogant in their hearts,
The oppressor who maketh the land to cry,
The ruler who is far from the peoples,
The ardent lover of God,
The pursuer of fleeting pleasures;
Yea,
None shall be spared.

Shall the offering of flowers
In the temple
Bring to thee the lasting comfort
That thou seekest?
Shall the chanting of many voices
Chase away from thy heart
The shadow that covereth it?
Shall the perfume of incense
Drive away from thy mind
The anxiety that over-layeth it?
Shalt thou forget the oppression
Of thy heart
By the consuming of drink?
Shalt thou chase away the shadow
By the company of many friends?
Shall the multitude of rejoicings

Bring to thee the consolation
That thou seekest?
Shall songs and music
Entice thee away
From thine affliction?
Shall the fleeting love
In its delight hold thee back
From thine aching heart?
O friend,
As the dark cloud
Blotteth out the sun
And casteth shadows on the land,
So in the days of laughter
Sorrow shall encompass thee about
And destroy the smile on thy face.

In the days of mine illusion,
When darkness lay about me,
I sought to overpower
The sorrow-laden heart
With the multitude of rejoicings.
Every abode of music knew me,
Every flower of decay held me,
Every jewel of the eye enticed me.
The cool temples,
With their great shadows
And the cooing of many doves,
Gave the passing comfort of a day.
The Gods thereof
Played with me
In the innocence of their greatness.
They whispered to me of the life
In the haven of their rest.
The preachers thereof
Lulled me to sleep
By the words of their books,
And the promises of reward
For my good deeds.

The perfume of the sacred flowers
Gave to me of their comfort.

As the leaf is
The plaything of the winds,
So was I the toy
Of sorrow.
As the cloud is chased
By the cruel winds,
So was I driven
From shelter to shelter
By the mutterings of affliction.

But now,
O friend,
I am beyond
The haven of the Gods.
The limitations of the preachers,
Of books,
No longer bind me.
As the soft breeze
That plays about the temple,
So have I become.
Not a thing shall hold me,
For sorrow is the companion
Of the seekers of shelter.
Yea, I have found
The eternal abode of happiness,
I have opened up
The fountain of lasting joy.
I am beyond sorrow,
I am liberated.

My Beloved abideth in me,
We two are one.

O friend,
I tell thee,
As behavior dwelleth with righteousness,
So eternal happiness abideth in thine own heart.

This vain search
After the desires of thy heart
Among the flowers of decay
Holds thee in its shadows.
Thou canst not escape
This fury of sorrow
In a moment of forgetfulness.
No God will give thee
The happiness thou seekest.
No mutterings of sacred words
Will loosen thee
From the cords of affliction.
There is no way
To that abode of lasting happiness
Save by the union of the self
With the Beloved.

Conceal not thy heart
In the sanctity of thoughtlessness
As the bird of prey
From the open skies
Examines the fields of the earth
For its food,
So thou must look into thy heart
And destroy the shadows
That are concealed therein,
For in the shade
Hides the self.

There must never be a moment of ease
Or the satisfaction of contentment,
For thou shalt not behold
The face of the Beloved
In a heart heavy with stagnation.
There must be revolt
And great discontentment,
For with these
Thou shalt purify thy heart.
Who shall give thee

Of these things?
Who will purify thee
Of thy stagnation?
Who shall uphold thee
In thy ceaseless struggle?
The perfume cometh forth
From the heart of the lotus.
O friend,
I tell thee
As behavior dwelleth with righteousness,
So eternal happiness abideth in thine own heart.

X

THE STRANGERS

At the great heights
Where the snow-clad mountains
Meet the blue firmament,
I met with two strangers.
We talked awhile
And separated,
Never to meet again.

As two ships,
On the vast waters of the sea,
Pass each other,
And the travelers thereof
Wave to each other,
Never to meet again,
So were we
On this sea of life.

Often
Have I felt sad
At the passing by
Of a stranger,
In some lonesome spot.
But yesterday,

When the two strangers
That I met with
Disappeared
Around the bend of a narrow path,
My heart went with them,
And they remained with me.

Of what nationality,
Of what faith,
I know not,
Nor care I.
They were like unto me,
Alone in a solitary place,
Seeking new visions,
Climbing greater heights,
Struggling up dangerous paths,
And going down to the valley
Once again.

This incessant struggle
To reach the mountain top,
Rarely attaining the glory thereof,
But ever descending
To the plains,
Where man makes his abode,
Has been my lot,
Life upon life.

But now,
O strangers,
I have reached the pinnacle
Of the mysterious mountain.
I know full well
The struggles thereof,
The great chasms that divide,
The precipices
That men
Slip down

I know full well
The multitude of paths
That encircle the mountain,
But they meet all
At the narrow ridge
Beyond which
All must climb upward
If they would attain
The mountain summit.

There is only one path
Leading upward
Beyond that ridge
Towards which all paths
Come together.

O strangers,
I know not
Where ye be,
Through what joys,
Through what struggles
Ye are passing,
But ye are myself.

As two stars
Of a sudden
Come into being
Of a dark night,
So ye two
Came into my vision
And there ye are established.
My heart is the heart
Of my well-Beloved,
It holdeth a multitude.

O my strangers,
Once again
Ye and I shall meet,
I dwell in the abode

Which is the end
Of all journey.
To be united with the Beloved
Is to love all,
For in all
Dwelleth the Beloved.

XI

THE SEARCH OF THE BELOVED

O friend,
I show the way
That shall open thy heart
To the welcome of thy Beloved.
As the precious metal
Is found at great depths
And for the discovery thereof
Thou must delve deep down
Into the heart of the world,
So thou must,
If thou wouldst behold
The face of the Beloved,
Dive deep within thy heart
And tear aside
The veil upon veil
That hides the glory,
The Light of thy life.

As a fire
Is covered o'er
With thick smoke
Before it shall burst forth
Into a roaring flame,
So, O friend,
Thy heart and mind
Are in a cloud of darkness
That can be dispelled

Only by the desire
Of thy deep purpose.

O friend,
Thy Beloved,
The desire of thy heart,
Is my well-Beloved.

In times past
There was a veil
That separated Him from myself,
But now
I have destroyed
This separation
And welcomed Him into my heart.
He abideth there
And I am consumed
With His love.

I tell thee
That my well-Beloved
Is the Beloved of all.
He and I are one,
We are inseparable,
Eternal and everlasting.
Yea,
I have found the way
That shall offer unto thee the ecstasy
Of purpose,
That shall unfold unto thee the beauty
Of life,
That shall give happiness
Unto all,
That shall bring unto thee the comfort
Of truth.

As the spark
That shall give warmth
Is hid among the gray ashes,
So, O friend,

The light
Which shall guide thee
Is concealed
Under the dust
Of thine experience.

O friend,
Wait not for the dark shadows
That shall fill the valley,
Cutting off
The sunlit view of the mountain,
For by the light of day
Thou canst see the path
That shall lead thee
To the great heights
Where the mists of life
Shall not confuse thee.
This is the time
When thou shouldst walk
In the open light.
The Beloved is with thee,
For He and I are One.

O friend,
As in the time of winter
Thou canst not sow the seeds
That shall give thee
The food for the coming year,
So in time of darkness,
Strife and confusion,
Thou canst not lay up
The lasting happiness
That shall be the wellspring
Of thy life.

O friend,
As in the springtime
When every seed
Shall shoot forth

To the glory of its fulfillment,
So in the days
Of thy great rejoicing
Every deed of thy thought,
Every action of thy feeling
Shall come forth
To its full fruition,
And it shall give thee
The burden thereof.

O friend,
As in the time of decay,
How sad it is
That the green foliage
Should wither and die,
So grievous it is
That in the time of desolation
There be none to deliver thee
From the shadows of thy creation.

O friend,
There is a time for all things.
This is the time
When thou shouldst walk
In the open light.
The Beloved is with thee
For He and I are One.

As a traveler
In the full knowledge
Of his voyage
Puts aside the things that shall weigh him down
On his journey,
So, O friend,
Set aside all things
That shall compass thee
On thy journey
In search of the Beloved.
For without the Beloved

There shall be no comfort
There shall be no rejoicing,
There will be no permanency
But
There shall be confusion,
Strife and the conflict of purpose,
A darkness and a searching,
A misery and a travail.

O friend,
The Beloved is thyself.
But to realize Him
And to hold Him
Fast in thy heart,
Firm in thy mind,
There must be no dark spot
Hidden away
In thy being.
No false comforters,
No pleasant Gods
Who give thee counsel
Of ease,
No greeds that bind thee,
No beliefs that shelter thee
In their dark shadows;
No thoughts, no affections that hold thee.

O friend,
Pursue the self
From shelter to larger shelter,
From temple to greater temple,
From desire to greater desire,
From conceit to greater conceit.
Mercilessly chase him
Down the paths of his delights,
Relentlessly question him
Of his dying certainties.
Till in the long last,
O friend,

Thou drivest him
To the open light
Where he shall cast no shadow,
Where he shall be united
With the Beloved.
Then thou shalt realize
The Beloved,
Then thou shalt be
Like unto myself.

O friend,
There is a time for all things.
This is the time
When thou shouldst walk
In the open light.
The Beloved is with me
For He and I are One.

XII

THE BELOVED IN ALL

My Beloved and I
Are one.
I come forth from Him,
My being is in Him.
Without Him I am
As the cloud that wandereth from one shelter
To another,
That hath no resting place.
In Him
Is my rest.
In Him
Is my glory.
For in Him
All things exist
And I in all.

O friend,
I tell thee
Of the way to the heart
Of the Beloved.
For I am the Beloved.
My Beloved and I
Are One.
As a dew drop
Entereth the sea,
So have I become one
With my Beloved.

The well-Beloved
Is in all.
All things are in the Beloved.
The blade of grass
That men do tread down,
The great spreading tree
That giveth shelter,
The green reptile
That men hold in terror,
The fly that annoyeth
The seller of the sweetmeat,
The singing bird
That delighteth the ear,
The fierce lion
That giveth fear
To the heart of the forest,
The simple barbarian
That men hold up in contempt,
The man of great knowledge
That giveth satisfaction to many,
The worshipper of many gods
That wandereth from shrine to shrine.

Life is one
As my Beloved and I
Are one.
There is only one way

To the heart of the Beloved.
That path lieth
Through thyself,
Through thine own heart.
Of that I tell thee.
There be many forms
Of His manifestation,
But there is only one way,
O friend,
That leadeth me
To the heart of my well-Beloved.

In times
When I obeyed
The laws of the gods,
Of the world,
I walked on the paths
That lead to their shrines,
And there
I was held in the power
Of their small authority,
But the fury of discontentment
Drove me on,
Never stayed I
In the shelter
Of the temple.
As one wandereth
From place to place
In search of lasting comfort,
So wandered I,
Setting aside the comforts
That gave me over to sleep,
Till in the long last
I opened my heart;
There found I
My well-beloved.

Many will tell thee,
O friend,

That there be various works,
Many ways
To the approach of the Beloved.
Yea,
There be,
But they all lead
To one path,
For there is only one way
To the heart of the Beloved.
Of that I tell thee.
If thou wouldst discover
My well-Beloved
That abides in me,
O friend,
Then thou must
Set aside all thy gods,
Thy comforts, thy small authorities.
Thou must cleanse thyself
Of thy conceit of little knowledge.
Thou must purify thyself
Of thy heart and mind.
Thou must renounce all
Thy companions,
Thy friends, thy family,
Thy father, thy mother,
Thy sister and thy brother.
Yea,
Thou must renounce all.
Thou must destroy
Thy self utterly,
To find the Beloved.

O friend,
Wouldst thou walk
In the light of a candle
When I give thee
The light of the Beloved?
I tell thee

My Beloved and I are one.
I know the way.
Come with me,
I shall lead thee
To my heart
Where dwells the Beloved.
There be many reflections
That fade and die away,
But I possess
The truth
That is everlasting.
Of that I give thee,
O friend.
Why is there doubt
In thy heart?
Art thou happy in the shadows?
Do men give thee
The substance that shall satisfy thy hunger?
Thou playest by the rivers
Of water,
But they quench not
Thy burning thirst.
Art thou content
With the decaying?

O friend,
My heart is heavy with love
For thee.
Come to me
And I shall give thee
Of my love,
That knoweth no alteration,
That knoweth no decay,
That withereth not,
For my well-Beloved and I
Are one.
I come from Him,
I tell thee

Of the way that lieth hid
In the heart of my Beloved.
I shall open unto thee
The gate
That shall admit thee
To the abode of my well-Beloved.
That valley lieth in the shadow
Of a deep cloud,
And I dwell among
The mountain tops.
Yea,
My well-Beloved and I are one.

XIII

I AM ALL

I am the blue firmament and the black cloud,
I am the waterfall and the sound thereof,
I am the graven image and the stone by the wayside,
I am the rose and the falling petals thereof,
I am the flower of the field and the sacred lotus,
I am the sanctified waters and the still pool,
I am the tree that towereth among the mountains
And the blade of grass in the peaceful lane,
I am the tender spring leaf and the evergreen foliage.

I am the barbarian and the sage,
I am the pious and the impious,
I am the godly and the ungodly,
I am the harlot and the virgin,
I am the liberated and the man of time,
I am the renunciation and the proud possessor,
I am the destructible and the indestructible.

I am neither This nor That,
I am neither detached nor attached,
I am neither heaven nor hell,

I am neither philosophies nor creeds,
I am neither the Guru nor the disciple.

O friend,
I contain all.

I am clear as the mountain stream,
Simple as the new spring leaf.

Few know me.
Happy are they
That meet with me.

XIV

I CANNOT TEACH YOU TO PRAY

I cannot teach you to pray, O friend,
Nor can I teach you to weep.
I am not the God of your long prayers,
Nor am I the cause of your many sorrows.
They are made by the hand of man.

Come with me, O friend,
I will lead you
To the fountain of Happiness.
Laughter is as the honey
In the heart of the scented flower.
You shall drink of it
In that garden of roses
Where all desire ceases
Save the desire to be like the Beloved.

This pool of Wisdom
Is not made by the hand of man,
Nor are the steps leading down to its clear waters.
There you will meet with every man,
The brown, the white,
The black, the yellow.

In its pure waters,
You will behold the face of my Beloved.

Come, O friend,
Leave all your passing joys,
Your burning anxieties,
Your aching sorrows,
Your fading love,
Your ever-growing desires.
For all these lead but to prayer,
To the cause of many tears.

As the passing wind is the life of man,
As the withering rose is the love of man,
The glory and the strength
Are gone in but a day.

I have drunk deep at this pool.
My Beloved has filled me
With the delights of eternity.

XV

TRUTH

Truth is neither evil nor good,
Truth is neither love nor hate,
Truth is neither the pure nor the impure,
Truth is neither holy nor unholy,
Truth is neither simple nor complex,
Truth is neither of heaven nor hell,
Truth is neither moral nor immoral,
Truth is neither of the God nor of the devil,
Truth is neither virtue nor vice,
Truth is neither birth nor death,
Truth is neither in religion nor without religion.
Truth is as the waters—it wanders,
It has no resting place.
For Truth is Life.

I saw the mountain come down to the valley.

XVI

Desire is Life.
The fulfillment of Life
Is the perfection of Desire.

As the scent of a lone flower is desire
That fades with the death of the flower,
That has no being in itself
But comes into rejoicing with Life;

As the roaring waters rushing through the dark valley—
Hidden, boisterous, terrible—
So is desire.

As angry as the waters seeking a release
Is desire.
Woe to him who is caught up therein.

Through the dark valley
Lie the open, smiling fields,
And the scent of many flowers.

The fear of desire
Is the putting away of Life.

XVII

In the corruption of the known
Man is stifled
By his fear of the unknown.

As a lone cloud is driven in search of a secluded valley,
So, pursued by fear,
Man creates out of the known
The protection of the image of God.
In that protection fear is multiplied.

Strange is the way of the shadow of fear.

The voice of fear calls out
And man burdens the earth
With the loveliness of a distant paradise
And with the horror of a near hell.
The shadow of fear covers the land.

Between himself and his fear
Man builds a temple for the image of his God,
And in its dark shadows is born a religion of great panoply,
Whose threat is conditioned by a loving priest.

Against that fear which he calls death,
Man seeks out a way for the furtherance of life,
And in that search fear is the master of his love.
The sacrifice of the unwise is out of the burden of fear.

The burden of wealth is the fear of the rich.
The poor are caught up in the desire for possession.
Envy, hatred, ambition, pride of dignity, judgment of convention,
The good, the evil, and the cruelty of binding morality,
Are but the sign posts on the path of fear.

If fear be the source of thought,
Then shall there be darkness in the land.
If the bubbling wellspring of love be corrupted by fear,
Then its clear waters shall create a burning thirst
In the mouth of man.

Ah, friend,
The loveliness of life is not the child of fear
But it lies in the womb of understanding.
Fear brings forth the tears of the world.
Laughter rejoices in the wake of true love.

A dried pool aches for the coming rains.

XVIII

Place not thy love in the scent of a decaying violet,
But hold in thy heart that love which is Life,
That love which is of the Beloved.
As a great flame that defies all corruption
So is this love of the Beloved.

O friend,
Why dost thou need the still weight of temples
When Life dances in the street?

O friend,
Why dost thou hide in fear—
Of death, of loneliness, of sorrow—
When Life rejoices about thee in the swaying fields?

O friend,
Why dost thou seek the passing comfort
When Life gives of its eternal understanding?

O, be the creators of great mountains
Rather than seek guides
To lead thee up their dangerous ways.

I am Life, I am the Beloved,
The flame that defies all corruption.

Ah, come with me,
Walk in the way of Life—
Love which brings no death.

XIX

O friend,
I am anxious for thee.

The long race with time,
The ceaseless dance with the winds of space,

The burden of lonely sorrow
And the gathering in of joy:
They are over, and I await thee
As the parched land the coming rains.

The love that corrupts the form of its loveliness,
Offerings to pacify the inward fear of thought,
Vain hopes void of understanding,
Visions and dreams ever in the semblance of man,
Death that creates darkness in life:
They are over, and I await thee
As the lotus the cool night air.

Hear me, O friend,
I await thee,
As the snowy peak in a still valley.

XX

In the choicest of valleys
There is moaning and lamentation,
In the great thoroughfares of men
There is the laughter of changing sadness,
In the melodious song
There is the emptiness of fulfilled desire,
Upon the lofty mountain
There awaits the stillness of death.

Wave upon wave
Comes the action of men
To break lonely upon the shores of vain glory.
The whirlwind of young love
Grows sad within the fold of a single day.
Thought conquers the great regions of time,
Only to return to the bondage
Of a deceiving mind.

Ah, desire is as young as the first ray of dawn,
And sad as the procession of death to the grave:

Struggle, the pursuit of fleeting pleasure,

Toil, the dull pain of easy ambition,

Gain, the gathering of the peculiar treasures of the rich,

Domination, the cry of perverted judgment that holds the heart of
    the oppressor,

Greed, the cruelty of privation that corrupts the growth of life,

Fear, the eager search after the shelters of comfort,

Worship, the deep forgetfulness from the confusion of many desires.

To the music of the distant flute

Flows the wide, ancient river,

Fresh with young waters.

Many chants are sung in praise of happiness,

Many gods are invoked as guides to happiness,

Many heavens are glorified as enticements to happiness,

Many altars are built to happiness,

Many rites are performed as offerings to happiness,

Many benedictions are asked as protection for happiness,

Many truths are extolled in anguish for happiness,

Many virtues are sought in fear for happiness,

Many possessions are gathered in hope of happiness,

Many desires are gratified in expectation of happiness,

Many sacrifices are made in quest of happiness,

Many austerities are imposed in longing for happiness.

Deep in the mire the seed of the lotus is in travail,

The soft fragrance lies hid in the heart of the flower.

XXI

Listen!

Life is one.

It has no beginning, no end,

The source and the goal live in your heart.

You are caught up

In the darkness of its wide chasm.

Life has no creed, no belief,
It is of no nation, of no sanctuary,
Not bound by birth or by death,
Neither male nor female.

Can you bind the "waters in a garment"
Or "gather the wind in your fists"?

Answer, O friend.

Drink at the fountain of Life.
Come,
I will show the way.

The mantle of Life covers all things.

XXII

As the potter's vessels break to pieces,
So are they broken who look for shelter,
For therein lie sorrow and ever changing confusion.
They that desire comfort
Shall find desolation.
Tears shall await those
Who have established comfort in the loftiness of their purpose.

I met a man in the shadow of a temple
And I beheld my face in his tears.

None shall wake thee from thy weariness
And the sun shall have arisen and set
Before thou walkest forth.
The fatness of thy heart
Shall blind thine eye in time of affliction,
And as a man is lost in the darkness of the forest,
So shall it be with thee
If thou stayest in the sanctuary of a graven thought.

Ah, friend,
Great must be the burning fire
To consume thy house of comfort,

To increase thy devouring anxiety,
For out of that confusion
Shall be born full understanding.

Take council with the whole
For in the part there is decay.

XXIII

There is order in the freedom of Life
But in bondage a great confusion.

Smooth as the waters that delight
In the burden of the pure eye of heaven,
So is Life in the fullness of its freedom.
Furious as the waters that are bound—
Filling the valley with deep anguish—
So is Life in the bondage of its confusion.

Let Life paint of its loveliness
On the canvas of thy being.
Be thou the background for its fullness.
And withhold it not its even flow.

He who walks upright amidst confusion
Is in love with Life.

XXIV

Ah, come sit beside me by the sea, open and free.
I will tell thee of that inward calmness
As of the still deep;
Of that inward freedom
As of the skies;
Of that inward happiness
As of the dancing waters.

And as now the moon makes a silent path on the dark sea,
So beside me lies the clear path of pure understanding.

The groaning sorrow is hid under a mocking smile,
The heart is heavy with the burden of corruptible love,
The deceptions of the mind pervert thought.

Ah, come sit beside me
Open and free.
As the even flow of clear sunlight,
So shall thine understanding come to thee.
The burdensome fear of anxious waiting
Shall go from thee as the waters recede before the rushing winds.
Ah, come sit beside me,
Thou shalt know of the understanding of true love.
As the mind drives the blind clouds,
So shall thy brutish prejudice be driven by clear thought.

The moon is in love with the sun
And the stars fill the skies with their laughter.

Oh, come sit beside me
Open and free.

XXV

To a man of true purpose
There is no renunciation;
For he is not drawn away from the path of pure understanding
By the confusion of experience,
By the multitude of desires,
By the deceitfulness of thought.

He is not held by the fear of sacrifice:
For the man of true purpose,
Time creates not its wasteful abundance.

I saw of an evening,
Over a city of vast habitation,
A bird swiftly flying towards its distant home.

XXVI

I walked on a path through the jungle
Which an elephant had made,
And about me lay a tangle of wilderness.
The voice of desolation fills the distant plain.
And the city is noisy with the bells of a tall temple.
Beyond the jungle are the great mountains,
Calm and clear.

In the fear of Life
The temptation of sorrow is created.

Cut down the jungle—not one mere tree,
For Truth is attained
By putting aside all that you have sown.

And now I walk with the elephant.

XXVII

POEM

The world moans and languishes,
Thought is ashamed and made crooked.
Love is a wilderness and a cruel confusion.
The pure blossom of Life is turned to dust.

How they suffer, how they despise!
The anger of contempt breeds hatred,
And affection is smitten in the midst of the street.
The shadow of weariness lies on the face of man.

His ambition is in the dust of decay,
His doubt creates a darkness about him,
His talk is as the sound of many hoofs
On the smooth-paved roads
Filling the silent house.

His glory, his pomp, his rejoicings,
Cover the empty spaces of his loneliness.
The dark fear of death
Snatches away the jewel in his eye.
And as the spider weaves with delicate ease its web
So man weaves the stuff of common events
But is caught up in its exquisite confusion.
His days are spent in the destruction of his handiwork.

The song of the river,
The wandering of the waters,
And a dead tree in full summer.

Ah, in the cruel confusion of purpose
The pure blossom of Life lies withering.
Who shall nourish it, who shall uphold it,
Who shall awaken it to its sweet fragrance?

My Beloved calls
And the echo goes aching down the valley.

XXVIII

THE GARDEN OF MY HEART

I am the path
Leading to the sheltered garden
Of thy heart,
O world.
I am the fountain
That feeds thy garden,
O world,
With the tears
Of my experience.

I am the scented flower
That beautifies thy garden,
The honey thereof,
The delight of thy heart.

Destroy the weeds
In thy garden,
O world,
And keep thy heart
Pure and strong,
For there alone
I can grow.

Create no barriers
In the garden of thy heart,
O world,
For in limitation
I wither and die.

I have a garden
In my heart,
O world,
Where every flower
Speaketh of thee.

Open the gates
Of thy garden of thy heart,
O world,
And let me in.
Without me
There shall be no shade,
Nor the soft breeze
From the cool mountains.

I have a garden in my heart,
O world,
That hath no beginning
And no end,
Where the mighty
Do sit with the poor,
Where the Gods
Do delight with the human.

Open as the vast skies,
Clear as the mountain stream,

Strong as the tree in the wind,
Is my heart.

Come,
O world,
Gather thy flowers
In the garden of my heart.

XXIX

Desire is life,
And the freedom of life is the freedom from desire.
Love is life,
And the happiness of life is the incorruptibility of love.
Thought is life,
And union with life is the glory of a boundless mind.

With the eternity of life,
Inseparable, undecaying and immeasurable,
I am in union:
Mine immortality is my Beloved,
The Beloved of all life.

XXX

O friend,
Sorrow is the flower of understanding
And it beareth the fruit of rejoicing.

Out of the fullness of thy heart
Invite sorrow
And the joy thereof shall be in abundance.
Sorrow shall bring forth love eternal,
Sorrow shall unfold the weaving of Life,
Sorrow shall give the strength of loneliness,
Sorrow shall open the closed doors of thy heart,
Sorrow shall conquer the spaces of eternity.

Out of the fullness of thy heart
Invite sorrow.
As the streams swell
After the great rains
And the pebbles rejoice once again
In the murmur of running waters,
So shall the gatherings by the wayside
Fill the emptiness that creates fear.

The scent is coming on the breeze.
Take not shelter
In the abode of authority
Where breed comfort and decay.
Come away, come away.
To go far,
Thou must begin near.
To climb high,
Thou must begin low.

The voice of sorrow is the song of fulfillment
And the rejoicings therein
The fullness of Life.

INDEX OF FIRST LINES

THE SONG OF LIFE

PARABLES

PROSE POEMS